Editor-in-Chief and Founder:
 Lyndon H. LaRouche, Jr.
Editorial Board: *Lyndon H. LaRouche, Jr., Helga
 Zepp-LaRouche, Robert Ingraham, Tony
 Papert, Gerald Rose, Dennis Small, Jeffrey
 Steinberg, William Wertz*
Co-Editors: *Robert Ingraham, Tony Papert*
Managing Editor: *Nancy Spannaus*
Technology: *Marsha Freeman*
Books: *Katherine Notley*
Ebooks: *Richard Burden*
Graphics: *Alan Yue*
Photos: *Stuart Lewis*
Circulation Manager: *Stanley Ezrol*

INTELLIGENCE DIRECTORS
Counterintelligence: *Jeffrey Steinberg, Michele
 Steinberg*
Economics: *John Hoefle, Marcia Merry Baker,
 Paul Gallagher*
History: *Anton Chaitkin*
Ibero-America: *Dennis Small*
Russia and Eastern Europe: *Rachel Douglas*
United States: *Debra Freeman*

INTERNATIONAL BUREAUS
Bogotá: *Miriam Redondo*
Berlin: *Rainer Apel*
Copenhagen: *Tom Gillesberg*
Houston: *Harley Schlanger*
Lima: *Sara Madueño*
Melbourne: *Robert Barwick*
Mexico City: *Gerardo Castilleja Chávez*
New Delhi: *Ramtanu Maitra*
Paris: *Christine Bierre*
Stockholm: *Ulf Sandmark*
United Nations, N.Y.C.: *Leni Rubinstein*
Washington, D.C.: *William Jones*
Wiesbaden: *Göran Haglund*

ON THE WEB
e-mail: eirns@larouchepub.com
www.larouchepub.com
www.executiveintelligencereview.com
www.larouchepub.com/eiw
Webmaster: *John Sigerson*
Assistant Webmaster: *George Hollis*
Editor, Arabic-language edition: *Hussein Askary*

EIR (ISSN 0273-6314) *is published weekly
(50 issues), by EIR News Service, Inc.,
P.O. Box 17390, Washington, D.C. 20041-0390.
(703) 777-9451*

European Headquarters: E.I.R. GmbH, Postfach
Bahnstrasse 9a, D-65205, Wiesbaden, Germany
Tel: 49-611-73650
Homepage: http://www.eirna.com
e-mail: eirna@eirna.com
Director: Georg Neudecker

Montreal, Canada: 514-461-1557

Denmark: EIR - Danmark, Sankt Knuds Vej 11,
basement left, DK-1903 Frederiksberg, Denmark.
Tel.: +45 35 43 60 40, Fax: +45 35 43 87 57. e-mail:
eirdk@hotmail.com.

Mexico City: EIR, Sor Juana Inés de la Cruz 242-2
Col. Agricultura C.P. 11360
Delegación M. Hidalgo, México D.F.
Tel. (5525) 5318-2301
eirmexico@gmail.com

The Land-Bridge and The World Crisis

EIR Contents

www.larouchepub.com Volume 43, Number 14, April 1, 2016

EIRNS/Doug DeGroot

Cover This Week

Hussein Askary (2009) in front of the Merowe Dam then under construction in Sudan, built in collaboration with China.

I. A Lesson for Us All

Editorial

Here are paraphrased excerpts from Lyndon La-Rouche's discussion with the LaRouche PAC Policy Committee on March 23.

Few Americans are untouched by the suicides of our fellow-citizens, especially those who should be our most productive workers. Whether suicides *per se* or through drugs or alcohol. You have to understand these kinds of things; you cannot put them at a distance; you have to get the full blast of what happened. And then, once you have done that, now you can be expiated under those circumstances, and say, yes, I've understood what the issue was, I've understood what the problem was, I've understood what the solution has to be.

There is not really the kind of attachment, even of the members of my own organization, of the type one would think would be appropriate for people who are very serious about life. And, therefore the seriousness of human life is something that has to be fully appreciated, otherwise you lose something of yourself. Otherwise you lose the ability to make good judgments.

There's no simple solution: as long as Obama and people like him exist as dominant forces in government, that's going to continue. Just think of the death-rate which is being imposed upon people who were actually formerly professionally employed. And they were just destroyed, or driven into suicide. And that has been going on, and those kinds of conditions are going on now. And that's what the characteristics of the United States are now, that kind of behavior, and nothing much is being done about it. And the Congress is not particularly useful in this area right now. So it can be addressed, but the question is, what are we doing about it? What means do we have to actually to do something to make this effective? And I say, right now we have almost nothing. We have the edges of things, but not really. We don't have a mission-orientation which will stick. We can probably intimidate people in their consciences about it, but that's about it.

Kesha Rogers of Texas intervened: "The purpose of the space program is to give a purpose and a mission to society. Right now, people are in effect being forced to take their own lives, because the society has taken their life from them. We see this in healthcare. People face this all the time. But as you have said, the real focus must be: What is the purpose and meaning of life after the person is dead, so that you're changing society to have a different conception of a love for human beings, rather than saying, 'Oh, that person is gone now.'"

Kesha continued: "The space program is no question of a small program of a few people. The achievements of the space program impact all of humanity for all time, as Neil Armstrong understood when he stepped onto the lunar surface, and said 'One small step for a man, one giant leap for mankind.'"

Lyndon LaRouche commented: "Remember that Obama is the enemy. Our mission is to get rid of Obama. He shut down the space program, and caused many other of these consequences with his bizarre behavior. Don't worry about Trump as such: get rid of Obama. That would change everything: like changing the diaper at last."

Let's look at it objectively, that is from a broader standpoint. These people are committing suicide, or destroying themselves in effect. Are we allowing that to happen? We're not allowing it, you would say: yet we're not doing anything to prevent it from happening. That's where the problem comes in. Are you producing the solution for the problem?—that's the issue. Every part of the United States, more or less, is afflicted with an increasing accumulation of people who are in desperate condition, either implicitly or implicitly. Those who are known to be deprived, are deprived,— but those who are experiencing the effect of that deprivation of others, are also deprived in that way. That's the kind of problem that we have to deal with.

What we need to do: You have to get mankind, himself, to understand: What's wrong with Obama? Well, Obama is Satanic. That's not an exaggeration; his character is Satanic. Everything about him is more than Satanic, in effect. And yet we tolerate that. People say they support the President, when he's a Satanic figure. And he goes around running Satanic operations. And they're not impressed; they're not sensitive.

So you get the person who says, "Oh, it's so sad, he died, he committed suicide, because he was depressed." What about what could have prevented that from happening? That's where the crime comes in. People will say, "Oh, it's too bad that people are suffering like this," but they're not going to do anything about it. That's where the problem lies. Because if you can't get a people that will muster themselves up to accomplish things that are necessary for themselves, then it doesn't work. We do have a weakness in this area; it's not our weakness as such, but we do share the burden.

There's no doubt of the consequence that's implicit in our Manhattan concerts and events. And what we have to do is get an estimate of the situation in other parts of the United States. What Kesha Rogers is doing, works. And she's become more conscious of her role of leadership. We need more of that in more parts of the United States. People come to the rescue, but they don't come fast enough. Since I went to prison, my own organization has not really been responsive to this, because some went to prison, and some sloughed it off.

If you want to make it work, you often have to spread it. You can't just make it work; you have to spread the process of reaction of that type. Then, other people get more into it: it works. Otherwise, you're looking at the aroma, not the substance. Something of that nature, you have to get it into your gut, to resonate. Which is the meaning of Manhattan. We need more of that. Otherwise, people around you who are frightened or suffering, they'll realize you're brushing it off. That "brushing-off" process is accumulating throughout the United States. And we have to bring forth a sense of concern, of serious concern for mankind.

Look at the history of Franklin Roosevelt's policy and practice. The issue is there. Because the struggle Franklin Roosevelt actually had, directly and indirectly as well, was a very striking, very important development. Then, when you got to 1936, coming out of the earlier 1930s, people began to get suddenly inspired with optimism, a growing optimism,— until the FBI destroyed Franklin Roosevelt's program while he was still alive and in office. The FBI was the agency which destroyed the morality of the United States, no one should forget that. The FBI is the dirty enemy of the United States and its principles. Now, we're come to a time in which the FBI is no longer really useful; there's nothing useful about it. And therefore the time has come, that we have to change the law to bring back the Franklin Roosevelt tradition. And therefore we are going to move joyously into doing things which mankind has not done for a long time. And that's what builds morality, what we should really call morality. A devotion to the progress and success of mankind. And we don't have that nowadays; we lost it a long time ago. The idea of building something that's going to make the whole field better; that's what Franklin Roosevelt's movement represented, and that's what we have lost, largely, in the United States today.

Are we doing it? Are we actually practicing that approach, or are we talking about it? I think it would take relatively little effort to make that shift. All you have to do is start it; all you have to do is get the thing started, and others will respond. Because people surrender to a sense of, "the way things are." They say "yes that's true, but, you've got to think of the way things are."

What we're doing in Texas right now, is really very important in that way. It's one way of getting the message across, by taking one area of work, and pushing that to be the infectious agent for changing the trend. What we really need right now, is an affirmation that these changes that we threaten to bring about, will function. When people get ignited with the fact that they have rights, rights that they thought they had lost, that's when you get the kind of ignition we need now in the United States. Without that, I don't think the United States can make it.

The main thing is to try to get the idea of an organization which is committed to victory, like a military organization, which gets out there and gets the job done. Texas can be one of the ignition points; Manhattan is another area of opportunity.

Physicians Who Are Not Permitted To Save Lives

by an experienced American physician

March 27—The unnecessary difficulty doctors now face in preventing suffering and saving lives has several sources, no one of which alone explains the totality of the problem. Everyone is aware of the routine denial of diagnostic procedures and treatment by insurance companies, as well as the non-continuity of care caused by changing contracts.

Also common is that medication coverage is often limited to medications outside those prescribed, while pricing practices are used to control the availability of drugs and devices. It is glaringly obvious that the immoral valuation of money before life can explain all of these situations. However, there is also a deeper side to this story.

Sworn to the Hippocratic Oath, each individual physician is personally responsible to follow the principle of life and alleviation of suffering above all else—a moral principle placing the patient above all other considerations. It is the individual physician who diagnoses and treats in the name of this principle. While science is one tool toward this goal, today this has been turned on its head.

The physician has now become the servant of a particular definition of science, one which is uninterested in the process of life. This is a new "life-detached" cold science, mathematically expressed by probabilities, statistics—superseding the commitment to life by imposition of adherence to guidelines based on statistical probabilities. Math before reason, math instead of cognition, chance before causation—this is population-control medicine, rather than life-pro-cess principled medicine. Denying causation, the physician sees his actions as not producing the patient outcome, but as submissive to Chance as expressed by a patient/physician detached numerical probability.

It is impossible to ignore the rising death-rates across the board reported by the CDC recently. Is this the result of all of the above? Was this imposed on medicine deliberately, and to what purpose? Such a question raises the issue of causal intent, rather than attributing this circumstance merely to Chance. Was the submission of physicians to mathematical cold science the result of conformity to popular opinion? Is a statistical probability a type of numerical popular opinion which denies man's cognition and his morally principled actions, and sees the physician and patient as mere beasts or billiard balls, rather than intertwined in creatively improving the process of life?

The Hippocratic Oath morally commits each physician to place the patient above all other considerations. Today, probabilities and statistical guidelines have replaced that Oath, while death-rates rise. Here, Hippocrates is depicted refusing bribery by Artaxerxes, in the 1792 painting by Anne-Louis Girodet de Roussy Trioson.

KESHA ROGERS

New Meaning to Why People Have To Live

The following remarks are taken from the March 23, 2016 LaRouche PAC New Paradigm Show:

Kesha Rogers: I think that we must look at where we are today from the standpoint of the degeneracy in the culture and the fact that the sense of optimism that was really the basis of what President John F. Kennedy set into motion has really been ripped from the population. The U.S. cultural collapse is the result of the continual attacks on real creativity and real science.

This has now been magnified by the collapse of the trans-Atlantic system.

I think that we can look at where we are today from a clinical standpoint, understanding the significance of the fact that today is the thirty-third anniversary of the Strategic Defense Initiative developed by Mr. LaRouche.

What that really represented was a continuation of the vision of President John F. Kennedy, because the intention of that policy was what Kennedy had set in place, which provided a mission for mankind to come together in the common interest of mankind. It wasn't merely just to set foot on the Moon, to land a man on the Moon, and only that.

Think about what President Kennedy had introduced: He understood that we had to actually create new frontiers of scientific development. He talked about producing satellites and nuclear power. A lot of people don't even remember that this was the vision of Kennedy, that we had to actually go much further with our investigation into the Moon, and then to

President John Kennedy launched the Space Program to provide a purposeful mission for mankind. Obama's decision to shut down the Space Program has contributed to denying a human identity to the population, leading to the present demoralization and degeneracy.

make these breakthroughs and new frontiers in scientific development that were going to actually change the paradigm and change the direction from what had been seen earlier with Truman: The collapse, and the attack on the FDR policy.

The same thing actually took place later with the policy of attack against Mr. LaRouche after he had gotten President Reagan to adopt the Strategic Defense Initiative. You look at this, clinically, from the standpoint of what we're seeing today with the insanity of the Bush-Obama policies to continue to put nails in the coffin of the real economy of the nation, driving the entire nation into utter collapse, and to instead represent the imperial policy that goes against what our nation was founded on, the identity which was put forth with a sense that we had a mission to fulfill, which was our destiny, especially under President Kennedy.

One of the things I'll just make note of right now is that you're seeing just how much this has completely demoralized our society. You have a society that has actually committed itself to death, a culture of death that is killing people, a culture where people don't see that they have a future, a future they can actually define. Why has this come along?

Well, it's been since the assassination of President John F. Kennedy, and since the jailing of Mr. LaRouche, and the shutdown of the Apollo Mission, and the shutdown of what was to be the continuation of that, through the Strategic Defense Initiative, that this demoralization has developed.

Now you're seeing the

long-term effects of that. I just attended the 47th Lunar and Planetary Science Conference. These conferences are held every year, so this shows you that the conference has been taking place, focusing on lunar and planetary exploration since the Apollo Mission. A lot of the people at the conference were crucial and key in the development of the Apollo Mission. There were also many young people there. It was heavily focused on the Moon, and what struck me about it, is that obviously, since the shut-down of the Constellation program by Obama and Obama's attacks on the space program, on the policy of going back to the Moon, that that policy has been eliminated.

Now what kind of mission, or what kind of vision do these people have? You had a sense of real demoralization and hopelessness that had set in, or people were really angry about the fact that they worked all of their lives based on the conception that we had an obligation, the mission to return to the Moon. But it got deeper than that. I also think that people are recognizing that it's our obligation to, as a scientific community, actually give people a sense of what it is that we are actually contributing to the further progress of humanity.

One of the things that came up, and we can discuss this more, is the fact that in 2008-2009, as a part of the rolling out of the Constellation program, prior to the Constellation being shut down by Obama, you had what was called the Lunar Reconnaissance Orbiter (LRO) that was put in place to orbit the Moon, to actually show a direction, with the intention of possibly organizing getting back to the Moon,— but that was never realized. Today, the LRO is still sending back spectacular images of the Moon, but the mission for a planned manned return to the Moon was shut down by Obama.

The key thing right now, is that what is missing in the discussion is a fight, not just over whether or not somebody thinks we should get back to the Moon. That's not the fight.

The real fight is that there has been a loss in our identity in the United States that we are acting on a mission for all of mankind. We have lost a sense of a national-international mission. And that is what people at the conference understood and started to really pick up on, as I was making certain interventions into the discussions about what China is doing.

And China is not just going to investigate the far side of the Moon, and is not only organizing a Moon mission because it is just something to do. What they are doing is to actually identify a new direction, a new paradigm for mankind, and are saying that this is going to benefit the future existence of man's identity and mission in space. And, obviously, everybody knows that the Moon is the first place for the launching pad for cislunar space,— the discoveries that are being made there, and will be made there, are going to benefit all of mankind.

We have to actually get a sense in the United States that the targeting of the space program by this President is completely unacceptable. He should have been, and must still be, removed, now! The reality is, we have to get people within the scientific community, as I've continued to state, to actually stand up and fight, because this is what is at stake.

The Mission for Mankind

Megan Beets: I had just re-read Krafft Ehricke's essay, *The Extraterrestrial Imperative,* and right at the beginning, he says, "The way to solve problems is to forge concepts which permit one to look beyond the problems," which I think is just a beautiful way of thinking about that, that you actually have to put your stake in something which is beyond the current system, which is ahead of the current system,— which is only something that mankind can do.

Rogers: It was interesting at this conference, that there is this urge and eagerness for this human identity, that people know that this is what they got involved in. It's not just about people's pet peeves, as though they are actually presenting high-school science experiments to show off or something. But, they know that what these scientific breakthroughs represent is a contribution to further advance and change all mankind.

This actually came up from one of the scientists at the conference, who was saying that NASA has a responsibility to work with other nations. It has a responsibility to recognize itself as not just a U.S. internal operation that's making some scientific experiments on the side. Rather, what we do is going to benefit and affect the progress of all mankind. Also, scientific discoveries that are made by other nations are not just going to benefit those nations, but they are going to benefit the existence of our nation,— as in the example that one of the scientists used in remembrance of the Apollo Mission, that when Neil Armstrong stepped on the Moon, he said that it was *"One small step for a man, one giant leap for mankind."* But that giant leap, everybody knew, had to continue—that the breakthrough and the optimism that was achieved with that was not to end there, it was to move forward.

You think about the threat that we are faced with right now: The threat to the existence of mankind coming from a British imperial system; A collapsing trans-Atlantic system, A collapsing Wall Street system that has to be brought down. You think about how far away we have gone from President John F. Kennedy's vision.

Instead, we see today the threat of war, as nations are being pitted against each other, instead of actually fighting to achieve the common aims of mankind. People should go back and really reflect and look at President John F. Kennedy's first inaugural address, where he speaks on the threat that was posed against the powers of the United States and the Soviet Union, or Russia.

This question still stands today. People have to say, let's put our differences aside, as John F. Kennedy did. We have a mission for mankind. He said:

> Let both sides seek to invoke the wonders of science, instead of its terrors. Together let us explore the stars, conquer the deserts, eradicate disease, tap the ocean depths, and encourage the arts and commerce. And let both sides unite to heed in all corners of the Earth the command of Isaiah, to "undo the heavy burdens, and let the oppressed go free.

How do you do this? How do you free people? Well, you free people by giving them a sense of human identity, that we have a mission as human beings to discover mankind's role in coming to know better who we are as human beings. The best way to do that is to go out into space. To go out and to come to know what is out there, what we can actually learn and discover—to actually explore the Universe. We have a mission in the Galaxy, and that mission is being stifled right now. It's being stifled by war; it's being stifled by economic collapse, and being stifled by Obama. So all those things that President Kennedy put forward, the way you are going to eradicate disease, and green the deserts, and so forth, is by going out and investigating the Galaxy.

Ben Deniston: Much of the general population gets a lot of propaganda about "China this, China that." Anybody who's serious, knows China is where things are going on. Education, science, development, investment in new technologies, the space program, infrastructure, nuclear power, rail, water development—you can go on and on and on. This space program is kind of

typifying it. Kesha, you are saying that if we want a future, if we want to actually be human, these are our allies. They're not attacking us. We have an insane person in the White House, following the orders of a dying Imperial system. That's the problem. We have an ally there that we should be working with in China. And yes, space is the place to do it.

Rogers: I think this question that Mr. LaRouche continues to get back to,— as far as the commitment, and the understanding of mankind, and human beings, and Americans, that we have an obligation to be actually acting for the future—that is what has been taken away. Why do we make new discoveries? Why do we make new breakthroughs? We are not making the breakthroughs so that somebody can feel comfortable, or can say that something is happening that's going to improve their immediate conditions and their immediate lives. Some people say, well, what is that going to do for me? How is that going to do something for me right now? This is backwards thinking in terms of economics. The method of LaRouche's economics has been to actually drive an advancement for the progress that is going to actually impact future generations that haven't even been born yet. Think about it from the standpoint of the destruction in society today, where people are reduced to thinking about the individual, "me." What am I going to get out of this? How am I actually going to survive, myself? There is no conception, and no commitment to what is it that we're actually doing to better and further the progress of future generations. You've lost that in society. So, now, you have a situation where you look at the conditions of the young people in society, they have come out of a generation, and they're continuing to be told, "well, you're just on your own. You are going to have to deal with this collapsing society, and this mess."

We don't have to deal with it in that way! This is the older generation to the younger generation. The key thing is that we have lost this identity of a commitment to those not yet born, to identify a future for them, as the grandparents used to state to the grandchildren— "I built this for you." Or, those people who didn't even get a chance to meet the next generations, who may have died beforehand, had a sense that they were leaving something that was going to, as I said, better the progress. So, that's what we have to get back to. That's the identity that has to be restored in a mission for mankind, that would be exemplified through the space program, as a key component of that.

Global Cooperation for the Future

Deniston: And we've got our insane President looking for asteroids to go jump onto. We've got this total joke of a program that's part of the destruction of NASA, on this crazy wild goose chase, on this supposed asteroid mission, which is going nowhere. We need to get a shift, and this is where we want to go. This is the next target.

Rogers: It really requires that there is a change in the identity and the thinking of the American people. Take the scientific leadership: They have to be the start of that change. They have to overcome and be rid of this fear that says that they have to go along with these insane policies, when they know that it is an attack on real creativity, real science, and on a commitment to a driver that's going to further the progress of mankind.

People are asking, how are we going to inspire the population? How are we going to bring a sense of optimism back? That was the subject of discussion that came up many times with some of the participants in this conference. They know that there is no sense that the role of the scientific community in the United States should inspire the population with an idea that they are participating in something great. So, they have a responsibility, and that is why we are actually fighting with these scientific leaders, to come together and recognize that we have to define a new direction for the space program, with what we could be doing if we were acting to collaborate with China, with Russia.

Yes, I know that there is an idiot policy in the Congress that says we can't work with China. Well, kick the idiot Congress members out that say this. The scientific community has more power, and more clout, over the idiot Congress members who don't know one single thing about science or about where the direction of mankind should be going.

That's a further subject of discussion, but I think this question of the attack on the scientific community, the fear that has set in, and the fact that you have taken away the ability to really do what we are passionate as human beings about doing, about making discoveries, about being creative—people are just frustrated by the fact that they have to go through all the bureaucratic insanity, and that they have to go along with what is forced upon them.

But they shouldn't accept that any longer. One thing I do want to say is that this is going to be the nature of the upcoming conference that is going to be held on April 7,

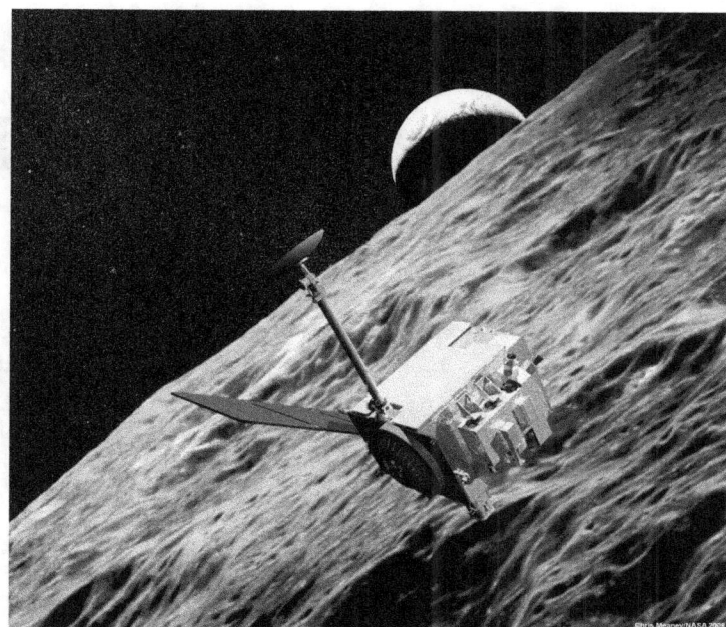

NASA/Chris Meany 2008

The Lunar Reconnaissance Orbiter was put into orbit around the Moon before the planned return of Man to the Moon was shut down by Obama.

and that we have to bring the best minds and thinkers within the scientific community, within the international community, together to say, let us map out a new course of direction for mankind, as we are seeing with China, with Russia leading the way right now. The United States has an obligation and responsibility to join in this effort, because if we don't, it will soon be too late.

Either we are going to go down with a collapsing, dying, system, or we are actually going to join with that new direction, in the course that's being set forth for mankind, one that is going to actually give new hope, new meaning, for peoples' lives, and actually give people a sense of why they should want to live, and that they might have a purpose to live, and an obligation and a mission to live, because what they are living for is going to continue to bring a new sense of direction, a new sense of meaning for those who come after them. So I think we have a big job in front of us, and looking at some of what we have said here, in terms of the demoralization, the people who are taking their lives— this is the discussion that Mr. LaRouche brought up.

We have an obligation to bring a new meaning to why people have to live, and why people have to have a sense of life, from the standpoint that we as human beings represent something that no other animal could ever achieve, or could ever do. So that should give us hope and happiness.

Some Things Have To Be Fought At All Cost!

The following excerpts have been taken from the March 26, 2016 Manhattan Dialogue with Lyndon LaRouche.

Question: Hi Lyn, it's A— here in New York. This week, what I wanted to bring up with you will stem partly from the statement you put out on "A Lesson for Us All" [see Editorial, page 4], and this is as it pertains to the continuing work to build up the conference on April 7.

Now in talking to people in the forty-year age-range, I'm uncovering something completely different, and I wanted to talk with you about it. Overall, although they appear to agree with things and understand that things are bad, really, there is this fixation or this slavish devotion to money. This is very ironic, because this is the same age-group that is being destroyed nationwide, although here in New York they seem to be so insulated or lack such compassion that they aren't moved by very much! I find the older generation depressed, demoralized, pessimistic; but *these* guys and gals—it's funny, they all say that there are two things that they believe in: sex, and money! And they're very up-front about that.

There is this generational difference that I'm encountering more and more, and I'd like to hear your response to this?

LaRouche: Well, essentially, there is no real difficulty in what you're saying in terms of this thing. It's *worse!* [laughs] You are understating the problem.

But the point is, what? We have a process of *destruction.* Now, how did this happen? *Bertrand Russell.* The degeneration of the United States was set into motion by British interests, by Bertrand Russell. He was the evil bastard who started the whole operation. What happened was, with each generation that was coming into the 20-year interval of age-group, they became worse, and worse, and worse, and worse, and worse. Because what had come out of the influence of Bertrand Russell on the United States culture, as well as on the British culture, was systemic degeneration. What you are seeing now, the effects that you're seeing,— for example, let's take all the people we know about who lost their position or were deactivated, and they degenerated.

They committed suicides, in one way or another, that is what has happened. Who did it? The British Empire, that's who did it.

And the point is, we are at a point now, where the implication for the United States is: *crush* everything that resembles the British system; crush it now. And don't forgive the French whores, either. They're abundant.

Europe is being corrupt itself, by its own corruption.

PRNewsFoto

The systemic degeneration of the United States was set in motion by British interests, by Bertrand Russell. Here, a team member during the World Cyber Games CounterStrike final.

To deal with trans-Atlantic corruption and degeneration, a great change will be necessary which will be located in places like Russia and China. Here, the pressure vessel of a high-temperature gas-cooled reactor is being installed March 20 at the Huaneng Shidao Bay nuclear power plant in China's first fourth-generation nuclear energy system.

Xinhua/Guo Xulei

It gives way to corruption! So what has happened now? We find out that the entire system, since Bertrand Russell, from his appearance into the present time,— the United States as we have experienced it heretofore, requires a great, sweeping change. Because if you're looking at what you are seeing in the population of living persons in the United States, they don't have the mental power to understand what the purpose of mankind is.

And therefore, the thing has come to a point in time, there will be a great change. And the great change will be located in such places as China, Russia, and other locations, outside the trans-Atlantic community. And what is in process now, is the survival of the United States and what it had represented, depends upon that change right now. It's going to be a tough change, but you look at what is happening to the people: Take three generations, 20 years each of these generations. You see the degeneration is immense, and there is only a tiny part of the entire U.S. population which has any comprehension of what the intention had been of the United States as we knew it. It's degeneration.

So we are fighting against degeneration, and we are looking for allies, or points of views of people who will create something new. Look at all the people who have been deprived of the kind of mental life they should have had. They're degenerating; they are committing suicide, of all kinds.

So what we have to do is, we have to really take the opportunity, because right now, on the edge of this moment, on this moment itself, the United States as an organization is on the edge of a general collapse. Now the only thing we can do from here, is to take what we have from the inside of the United States that still has some element in it, and recognize the fact that we are going to a great crisis, a great financial crisis which is due to come very soon, but when that crisis comes upon us, and it will, there won't be much left in the United States, of power, unless we can intervene, with help from abroad on this issue, and we can restart what was once the United States.idea?

[Follow-up] We will intervene. Thanks, Lyn.

How Can You Reach Them?

Question: Mr. LaRouche, I come from California. I wanted to ask you, how does one deal with resistance in terms of Russia and China. There are good people that I run into all the time; they say, "Oh! You can't...! They're dictators!" They won't have anything to do with it. So I'm finding it really challenging to come forward and to organize through the music—which I was very, very, very touched by your reference in one of your latest talks about the epidemic of suicide, you know, through alcoholism and drug addiction, which is just the attempt of people to counter their fear, to connect with their spirits, their soul! As one fellow said this, the director of my Shakespeare company said, his favorite poem is "Life is earnest, life is real, and the grave is not its goal. Dust thou art, to dust returneth, was not spoken of the soul."

And I think that's what the gentleman that just spoke was referring to, this common generation that all they want is sex and money, because they've lost that connection.

So I guess what I'm asking is, how would you go about reaching these people so that we're all on the same page, as it were?

LaRouche: Well, I would say, you want to look at

some great people from the past, and there were in that process great people, who come up out of, well, shall we say, the Renaissance period? And this was largely crushed in that period. The Catholic Church destroyed itself and was crushed in that period.

Then the Church itself tried to struggle for its freedom again, because the hatred against the religious codes at that time, really disgusted people. It was a sudden change, where people were actually cooked to death, for no reason whatsoever.

And then there was a great freedom, and various people created freedom, helped it, and the result was the creation of the United States out of this process. And we began to lose it again; we lost it again; we regained it. We lost it again, we regained it, we lost it again! And I think the last score—we lost it again. And that's the last thing on record so far.

But, if you have the understanding of what the issue *was,* what the issue *is,* you can use that understanding as a point of reference for organizing yourself and other people. And that's the answer.

Question: Hi Lyn. I'm from Montreal. I came down here to help organize the Manhattan Project. And I've been reading a book on Gestalt psychology, where Wolfgang Köhler talks about this idea of "radical subjectivity." So it's this kind of Bertrand Russell-like idea, where the only thing you can know for sure is what you take in through your senses. So how do you know if something's real, if you're not directly observing it? Or how do you know that other people are really sovereign and not just these types of automatons? It seems to me that most people, whether they're conscious of it or not, believe in this idea in some form, and they've become really self-centered, self-absorbed, and really focused on getting immediate pleasure. And this is especially in young people, especially in people my age.

So my question is, first, what are your thoughts on this? And how can we really get people out of their neuroses?

LaRouche: Well, most people get released when something goes their way. And usually what goes their way is what leads them into disaster! So that's the problem.

So therefore, you have to be really, truly objective. You have to say, "Well, look, what's the situation? What's the historical situation?" And I can tell you, the United States has no historical power to maintain itself.

It doesn't. There are some forces which are interesting, important; but at present, the victory does not lie with us. It lies with the tyrants, who dominate us.

Now, under certain circumstances, the reason I'm so nasty about some things is because I know that some things have to be fought, at all cost, because you cannot respect yourself, unless you fight that fight. And that's the answer, in short.

The Teaching Business

Question: Good afternoon. This is J— from Brooklyn. You have often talked about the purpose of mankind, and the idea of a future vision. That reminds me of what is necessary and how, as you just said, we must regain the United States.

I just want to go over a little bit about what happened to me this week, in one of my classes as a teacher. I'm a middle school teacher, but I was assigned to a second grade, because their teacher was sent out on a workshop. I'm not really familiar with the little ones, but this situation, I think you might find interesting.

I decided that since I got this class. and they are all seven, maybe eight years old, I would ask them what they would do if they were President? So, I said, "OK, little guys, if you were President, first of all, what does the President do?" And I got some really cute little answers, such as "well, the President helps people," and "the President makes laws."

Next I asked, "What if you were President, what would you do to make things better?" So, I'm going around checking out their answers, and I see that one little boy says, "well, if I was President, I'd be dead." So I say, "What do you mean?" He says, "well, the good Presidents are dead!" I said, "Well, what do you want to do?" He says, "You're supposed to help people, you're supposed to make sure that people have food; you're supposed to make people safe. You're supposed to make sure that people have a job." So I said, "where did you get this idea from?" He goes, "Oh, my grandpa!" And I said, "What President are you talking about that's already dead?" He goes, "FDR."

So if we do our job, and we make sure that we have a future for these little kids, these little seven and eight year olds, it instills in me, and I want to pass it on to everyone else, that we have to do this in order make sure that there's a future for these little second graders. And the way to do that is to do what we do, to keep doing what we're doing. And I'd kind of like you to

A Chinese-designed CRH380 high-speed train leaving Shanghai's Hongqiao Station.

creative commons/Khalidshou

comment on the idea of the future, and a vision of mankind and what will inspire all of us, like you always do, to work harder to make sure that even though that generation that is talking about sex and money is fading away, fortunately,— they won't be here forever,— but these little seven and eight year-olds are coming up, and that is our future. So if you could just comment on that idea?

LaRouche: OK, I'm going to give you a shocking—for many of you—a shocking exposition on what this issue is. The usual assumption is that children, once born, become the maker of the future. That is not necessarily true; it is not universally true. Why?

What is this silly idea, that a human being is born, grows up a little bit at least, grows up perhaps a little bit more; now, how does mankind progress? Well, somebody else gives them that progress. How does that progress come about? Well, the giving of that progress is something most people don't know how to do.

Now, you know, that this teaching business: Let's suppose that you come in there, and there are little children in this place, or somewhat middle-aged children, relatively speaking; and you find out that they develop. Is that what you wish to achieve? Is that adequate for you to achieve? Or do you have to create something about the new child. A newborn child who will be prompted into becoming a discoverer of the future.

Mankind's authority lies in the future. It lies intrinsically in the future. And we need children to be born who are not imitations of their parents. Because if you don't, you won't have a person who is creative, actually, individually creative, not practical! Practical people do not pass the test! It's only truly creative minds that allow mankind to make progress. But what happens whenever you lose that mind, you find that populations, such as that of the United States, degenerate.

And therefore, the question is, can you cause the development of children to become creative forces, even in opposition to their parents, and come back to their parents, and say, "I am bringing this home to you, share with me, as something new, that you, the parents, didn't know, or were not prepared to act on." And these people who have that quality are called leaders, rightly called leaders. If you can not be a leader beyond anything that popular opinion suggests, you are a failure for mankind.

Question: Hi Mr. LaRouche. My name is I— and I'm from Brooklyn. This is my first time being here, and I just want to thank you. You're a grandfather figure to me; I've always been watching you on the LaRouche PAC website, and you have helped me to understand that personal choices have to be right choices, no matter how unpopular. Because your views and principles in economics as a physical science, that man must control the noösphere, and that man is built in the image of God, to me are very inspiring, and I just want to thank you today.

My questions are, how do you stop? At what level of government can a simple citizen change and be active on a day-to-day operations?

LaRouche: We need to copy the reality of Einstein. Einstein is the appropriate model in all aspects, for what the future of mankind must be. And he gave a number of examples in the course of his life which demonstrated how *he,* as a creative mind, was able to bring

April 1, 2016   **EIR**   The Land-Bridge and the World Crisis   13

When Obama cut the space program, the minds of the people of the United States were crushed. Here, an artist's rendering of components of NASA's Constellation Program, a heavy-lift system which was to go to Mars and beyond, before it was cut. Shown is release of the cover for a lunar lander, and solid rocket booster separation.

mankind ahead, where the rest of mankind couldn't make it.

And that is what is important. The people who are creative people, who create things that mankind has not otherwise been able to create, and that's the standard. And Einstein is simply a symbol of the people who fit that kind of career in life.

[Follow-up] Could you help me out, in terms of, how do you break through in understanding new fields? What gives you hope?

LaRouche: Well, I find, first of all, hope comes from adversity. If you don't have adversity, if you're popular, you're probably not worth much. If you are able to create something that mankind has not yet otherwise provided, that is a success. And people who are smart, really smart, will try to achieve things that other people have not achieved. Why? Out of jealousy? No! Out of resentment against stupidity.

Question: Hi Mr. LaRouche, it's H— from New York. I've been talking to various housing activists at rallies and other places, including leftists, and Ameri-

can Muslims, and people in tenant organizations, and these people really need a flank because they're going nowhere. And I tell them that China has built sort of a subway system nationally, that is 11,000 miles long, and goes 200 mph, and this is what we have to get in touch with and be part of. And in many cases the response is very weak. They have hard time grasping anything international. But that's where we are.

LaRouche: The space program. When Obama cut out the space program, they destroyed, crushed the minds of the people of the United States. That is what the problem is. And look at the space program: Just go back and study who the people were who did the space program, who developed it. *This* was achievement. What happened? Obama! Obama *crushed* the United States! That was his mission. He killed people, he killed them on schedule, every Tuesday. He killed people. He's probably still doing it, because that's what he has done for a career.

So anybody who is nice to Obama, is a bad person intrinsically. You have to get rid of Obama and what he represents. Every step that Obama is President, that step is a step of treason against the United States.

Every Day Counts In Today's Showdown To Save Civilization

That's why you need EIR's **Daily Alert Service**, a strategic overview compiled with the input of Lyndon LaRouche, and delivered to your email 5 days a week.

For example: On Jan. 7, EIR's Daily Alert featured the British hand behind the pattern of global provocations toward war. Of special note is British Intelligence's role in instigating the Saudi Kingdom's attempt to set off a Sunni-Shia war. This religious war has been the intent of British strategy since the Blair-Bush attack on Iraq in 2003.

We also uniquely update you regularly on the progress toward the release of the suppressed 28 pages of the Congressional Inquiry on 9/11, which would expose the Saudi role.

Every edition highlights the reality of the impending financial crash/bail-in policies that would realize the British goal of mass depopulation.

This is intelligence you need to act on, if we are going to survive as a nation and a species. Can you really afford to be without it?

THURSDAY, JANUARY 7, 2016

Volume 2, Number 97

EIR Daily Alert Service

P.O. Box 17390, Washington, DC 20041-0390

- British Crown Pushing War and Genocide in 2016
- Financial Mudslide Goes On; Monetarist Tyranny Gloats over Bail-Ins
- Moody's Downgrades Portugal's Novo Banco
- Puerto Rico's Default: It's Every Vulture for Himself
- Wide Glass-Steagall Debate Set Off Again by Sanders Speech
- MI6 Mouthpiece Evans-Pritchard Touts Persian Gulf Chaos
- North Korea Tests a Miniaturized Hydrogen Bomb
- Uighur Terrorists Found in Indonesia
- Foreign Investors Are Flocking In to China

EDITORIAL

British Crown Pushing War and Genocide in 2016

II. Solving the Crises with the New Silk Road

EIR Seminar in Frankfurt on New Silk Road for Mideast and Africa

by Rainer Apel

FRANKFURT, March 23—The seminar, "Solving the Economic and Refugee Crises with the New Silk Road!" organized by *EIR* in cooperation with the Consulate General of Ethiopia in Frankfurt, Germany, was attended by an audience of 75, consisting of representatives of several diplomatic offices, subscribers and contacts of *EIR* in the region, and about ten Syrians (students as well as refugees waiting for enrollment at universities). Several contacts came from as far away as Berlin and cities in Switzerland. Extending over the entire afternoon, the seminar featured presentations by Helga Zepp-LaRouche, chairwoman of the Schiller Institute; Hussein Askary, *EIR* Arabic Editor, Stockholm; Mehreteab Mulugeta Haile, Consul General of the Federal Democratic Republic of Ethiopia; Marcello Vichi, former Director, Foreign Department, of the Bonifica company and author of the Transaqua concept; Andrea Mangano, Vice President, Italian Association of Water Engineers and contributor to the Transaqua outline. The speakers were joined by Mohammed Bila of the Lake Chad Basin Commission and Ulf Sandmark of the Schiller Institute Stockholm and Swedish-Syrian Committee for Democracy, for an expanded panel in the second part of the seminar. The seminar was moderated by Claudio Celani of the *EIR*'s European center in Wiesbaden.

In her keynote address, Zepp-LaRouche stressed that this would not be an academic seminar but rather a discussion about the fact that in this existential crisis of

EIRNS/Christopher Lewis

Helga Zepp-LaRouche, who led the conference, is flanked by Marcello Vichi, author of the Transaqua concept for rescuscitating Lake Chad (right), and Claudio Celani of EIR *Wiesbaden, the conference moderator.*

mankind, shown by the refugee crisis, the wars and the financial crash, solutions are within reach and must be realized now. In the wake of the terror attacks in Brussels yesterday, it is more than appropriate to recall former U.S. Senator Bob Graham's statement of mid-November last year after the terror attacks in Paris, that had the classified 28 pages of the Joint Congressional Inquiry into 9/11 been made public, such atrocities could and would have been prevented.

It is beyond any doubt that the Russian military intervention into Syria changed the rules of game, that it exposed the role of that pro-ISIS alliance of Saudi Arabia, Qatar, the United States, and United Kingdom, and particularly the role of Turkey, whose policies have

The conference on "Solving the Economic and Refugee Crises with the New Silk Road" was held in Frankfurt, Germany, in cooperation with the Consulate General of Ethiopia on March 23. Here, Consul General Mehreteab Mulugeta Haile reports to the conference Ethiopia's rapid development. Ethiopia is currently negotiating with Brazil, Russia, and India to finance and build rail links to Kenya, South Sudan, and Djibouti. China and Turkey are already partners for other routes.

been attacked harshly by two former U.S. ambassadors to Ankara. The European Union agreement with Turkey on containing the refugees is a travesty which fits into the general picture of Western and U.S. human rights violations, which have just been exposed in a Chinese dossier. While the West is talking about an insanity such as "helicopter money" to save its own speculative banks, the Chinese "One Belt, One Road" initiative presents an offer for a win-win strategy based on the real economy; that is, a strategy that is not just in the interest of China but also of the other nations—and real development only will help to dry out terrorism. Either Europe works with Russia, China, India, Iran, Egypt, and other nations to launch a Marshall Plan for Syria and Africa, or its bankrupt economies will crash against the wall, Mrs. Zepp-LaRouche said.

Presenting the *EIR* World Land-Bridge report in its first Arabic translation, Hussein Askary reported that as this seminar was being held in Frankfurt, an event presenting the Arabic report was also taking place in

Yemen that same day under conditions of continued Saudi airstrikes on Yemeni cities. The idea of the New Silk Road is more than just building a few roads and railroads; it is a concept of development corridors improving the life of some 450 million people in the Southwest Asian region, with Syria being at the center. This involves mega-projects of rapid development, financed by national development banks free of the obligation to pay unpayable debt as demanded by the Western monetarist institutions. Like Egypt, Syria will focus on industrial zones, transport corridors, and agricultural development, with China showing the way with its massive infrastructural engagement, for instance in East Africa.

Ethiopian Consul General Haile followed with a presentation on the economic strategy of his country, characterized by policies that have greatly improved per-capita income, literacy, and public health care since the 1990s. With an envisaged annual GDP growth of 11%, Ethiopia seeks to become a middle-income country by 2025, made possible by opportunities for Ethiopians to set up a farm or shop at the price that many pay today to human traffickers to be brought to Europe as refugees. Ethiopia itself is the largest refugee host in Africa, having taken in 800,000 refugees from South Sudan, Somalia, and Eritrea—a fact that no one in Europe talks about. Ethiopia will be transformed from a primary-products exporter to a nation with high-value production and infrastructure, and the country's cooperation with Russia, China, India, and Brazil in rail projects is important in this context.

Marcello Vichi then reviewed the history of the Transaqua Project discussion over the past 35 years, from the first proposals presented by Italy's Bonifica company in 1982-1985, to African governments and the UN pointing to a transfer of water from the giant Congo River as the only viable option for refilling Lake Chad. The proposal has largely been met with disinterest or pessimism as to the chance of its realization and has been discarded as allegedly "megalomaniac," but the recent refugee streams have made Europe rethink its views, and Transaqua, which has always meant more than just water for Chad—but is rather the broader framework for the development of all of Central Africa—is the only option that can attract the young generation of the African labor force, so that it will not become refugees.

Andrea Mangano then presented an overview of what Lake Chad was 35 years ago and what it is now, with 90% of its water lost. It shares the problem with other evaporating inland lakes in the world that are no longer supplied by their traditional tributaries—the Aral Sea (Uzbekistan/Kazakhstan), Lake Urmia (Iran), Lake Turkana (Kenya), and the Dead Sea (Jordan/Israel). The process is only reversed by water transfer and reduced consumption by irrigation using new technologies. This is what Transaqua does; it will tap 5% of the water from the upper tributaries of the Congo River, water that otherwise flows unused into the Atlantic Ocean in a volume fourteen times that of Germany's biggest river, the Rhine. Refilling the lake will be accomplished with infrastructure construction that will give the entirety of Central Africa hydropower, irrigation for agriculture, and waterway transport, and will relieve the region's present land-locked condition.

Mohammed Bila of the Lake Chad Basin Commission elaborated on the Transaqua issue in the expanded panel, pointing to the large and ongoing migration wave southwards from Chad since the great drought of 1973, during which Lake Chad lost 40% of its water inflow. The farmers and their cattle that have migrated to the south will not return to Chad unless the lake is refilling, and unless the terrorist movement of Boko Haram has been crushed.

Ulf Sandmark reported on his two visits to Syria in 2014 and 2015, during which it became evident that the reconstruction of Syria actually implies the development of the entire Southwest Asia region, making it an integral part of the New Silk Road—to which he found the Syrians open, and when the "Phoenix" reconstruction plan drafted in Stockholm was presented to the Syrians during the second visit, it received broad coverage in the country's media.

The panelists' discussion with the audience featured additional aspects of what was said in the presentations, including the genocidal tradition of the British Empire, which has sabotaged real development in Africa and the Mideast; the hopelessness of the monetarist system; and the increased threat of a thermonuclear world war if the chance to change course toward cooperation with the New Silk Road is not taken by Europe and the United States; and that we are in a race against time to enter a new paradigm before the total collapse destroys everything. It was raised that, contrary to Western black propaganda, China is not engaged in Ethiopia for raw materials, since Ethiopia has none, but instead is a real partner for development.

Zepp-LaRouche repeatedly insisted during the discussion that the participants of this Frankfurt seminar take home with them the commitment to set fire to the behinds of the policy makers to force a fundamental change, that a real mass movement for development has to be created. Vichi made a passionate appeal that there is good reason for optimism, and that the change requires that we work from that optimistic basis. A new and creative image of man, as it was developed in the great Italian Renaissance, is required also today, Celani pointed out. Sandmark insisted that the New Silk Road is not just for engineers, but for everyone to study at seminars and chapter meetings. The first chapter meeting on the Arabic language report in Yemen today was actually being presided over by the leading poet of that country, Askary added.

Solving the Economic and Refugee Crises with the New Silk Road!

I welcome you. While this seminar is devoted to solutions to the world's urgent problems, I must address the current dramatic threatening events very briefly. And I only want to emphasize, that while I'm touching on these different existential threats to our civilization, the solutions are within reach and depend entirely on our actions.

Thus, this is not an academic seminar, but really a call to move to implement the solutions we will present over the course of the afternoon.

Now, I think one can say that we have an existential crisis of civilization. If you look at all the different crisis spots and other crisis issues in the trans-Atlantic world alone, an honest person must admit that the human species is being tested:

- Refugee crisis
- Financial crisis
- War danger
- Cultural crisis.

Are we morally fit to survive? Are we intellectually able to grasp and seize the solutions which exist? Or are we doomed to continue on the present course which is heading towards disaster.

First, it is necessary to correct some of the explanations being presented in the public domain for these crisis issues.

Let me very briefly touch on what happened in Brussels yesterday, which obviously concerns everybody—the threat of terrorism. In response, governments are asserting that we have to give up data security, that we have to have more centralization, we have to give up freedoms.

Helga Zepp-LaRouche led the conference on "Solving the Economic and Refugee Crises with the New Silk Road."

And I would counter that with the statement made by the former head of the 9/11 commission of the U.S. Senate, Sen. Bob Graham [D-FL] after the attack on *Charlie Hebdo* happened more than a year ago in Paris. He said that if the famous [classified] 28 pages concerning the role of Saudi Arabia in the original September 11 attack had been published, this *Charlie Hebdo* terrorism would not have happened.

You cannot discuss what happened in Brussels and the threat of terrorism without looking at the role of Saudi Arabia and Qatar backing Wahhabi Salafism, as well as the fact that Turkey is buying oil from ISIS up to the present day, and is supporting ISIS with weapons and equipment.

The spokesman of the Russian Foreign Ministry, Maria Zakharova, just said yesterday that the double standard concerning terrorism has to stop. One cannot support terrorism in one part of the globe and not expect it to appear in other parts of the globe. Now, just to give you one example, on March 15—a couple of days ago—the Saudi-led coalition bombed a marketplace in Mustaba, in the northern Yemen, which killed 120 people, including 20 children, and wounded 80. This was not mentioned at all in the Western media. These people are just as human as the people in Brussels.

In light of what I have just said, the fact that the EU is putting all of its eggs in one basket, the deal with Turkey, to solve the refugee crisis is completely ludicrous. Even the former neo-con ambassadors of the United States, Eric Edelman and Morton Abramowitz, who both were ambassadors to Turkey, said that the Erdogan government does not function, that it's an authoritarian regime, economically collapsing, and conducting civil war against its own population, namely the Kurds.

The EU says that we have to solve the refugee crisis with a deal with that government, even though the UN High Commissioner already has said that the mass deportation of refugees now going on from Greece to Turkey is illegal.

This proposal had already been demonstrated not to work, because the day after this agreement went into effect, 1,662 refugees landed in Greece seeking new routes and new islands, since the refugees are very afraid of being sent back into the arms of ISIS.

In protest, the UN Human Rights Commission and the Doctors Without Borders have stopped working with the refugees because, they say, this approach is untenable and will not not work. The UN Human Rights Commission also said that the so-called hotspots [containment centers for refugees], which are supposed to solve the refugee crisis according to the EU, have been turned into detention camps. Families are not allowed to leave their homes, and they have *de facto* been turned into prisons.

The United Left of Spain is pursuing a criminal suit against Spanish Prime Minister Rajoy for condoning the EU-Turkey agreement, saying this agreement provides no help to the refugees, this is deportation of human beings who have the right to be at least checked to verify whether they have the right for asylum, and you cannot simply deport them.

Hungary is being attacked by the EU, and media there and elsewhere are raising the question: "What happened to the humanistic rights or values of the European Union?"

Our [German] President Joachim Gauck is presently on a tour to China. He has brought up the issue of human rights violations in China. This would be a farce if it were not so tragic for the people who are the victims of the EU policy.

Let me just say this on China: In response to the accusations of human rights violations, China issued its own report on human rights violations in the United States, including looking into the continuous wars in

Xinhua/Ju Peng

President Xi Jinping announced the One Belt, One Road mutual development policy two years ago while on a visit to Kazakstan. The initiative has grown dramatically since then. Here, President Xi Jinping (left) is standing next to his Kazakstan counterpart Nursultan Nazarbayev, during that 2013 trip.

the Middle East based on lies, and the drone killings, and concluding that it is ridiculous, in light of all of these types of activities, that the United States is still playing the role of the judge in the human rights case.

China, in its own right, has lifted 900 million people out of poverty. In my book, they have done more for human rights than anybody who is accusing them of violating human rights, because if you look at the EU and the United States in turn, where the rate of poor people is increasing all the time—in the United States it's 50 million and rising. One element of the new Five-Year Plan of China is to alleviate poverty in China by the year 2020, and worldwide by 2025.

So therefore, one needs to have a different view than that which is being presented by the media.

Now, let's look at a second "spin" or big lie. A big story is being spread that China is responsible for the financial turmoil in the markets, that the Chinese economy is collapsing, that the New Silk Road will be a flop.

By comparison, look at the situation in Europe. The European Central Bank (ECB) chief Mario Draghi not only set the interest rate at zero, negative interest rates for banks who want to park money in the ECB, but he is now openly talking about "helicopter money." "Helicopter money" means to just throw out money out [as if] from helicopters to flood the markets with liquidity. Even Otmar Issing, who is a staunch monetarist to my knowledge, the former chief economist of the ECB, said "this is a devastating idea. A central bank which is giving out money for free is hardly able to ever regain control of the markets. This is total mental disarray."

Now, fortunately, the lifeboat for the sinking *Titanic* of the European and U.S. economy is already there, provided by the New Silk Road offer of China—the "One Belt, One Road" policy.

This was proposed by Xi Jinping two years ago, in Kazakhstan, and since then has taken a dramatic development. There are now over 70 nations which have expressed concrete interest to cooperate with the Silk Road and over 30 countries have signed very concrete agreements on many, many projects.

The New Silk Road, for which the Schiller Institute has been campaigning for 25 years, as our answer to the collapse of the Soviet Union, is a completely different model. It's based on what President Xi Jinping called a "win-win" policy of that countries cooperating on joint projects on the basis of mutual interest, of complete respect for the sovereignty of the other nation. China is pursuing its own interest, but it is also providing what is in the interest of the participating countries.

Now, Foreign Minister Wang Yi just recently said "the New Silk Road is China's idea, but it creates opportunities for the whole world." And it is definitely the new model of relations among all countries. Chinese intra-Asian trade is now progressing with high growth rates. However, its relations with Europe and the United

Xinhua/Bao Dandan

China's Foreign Minister Wang Yi (shown here) said recently that "the New Silk Road is China's idea, but it creates opportunities for the whole world."

VOA

China's Premier Li Keqiang (shown here) speaking of internal improvements in the Chinese economy at the just-concluded National People's Congress, where the 13th Five-Year Plan was presented, said the goal is to transform the Chinese economy into a knowledge-intensive one. He mentioned innovation 61 times.

States are suffering, not because of China, but because of the economic and financial turmoil within the EU and in the United States.

The Chinese leadership's response to that is to turn a crisis into an opportunity, by advancing the internal Chinese economy into the next qualitative leap forward by innovating and creating new industries, upgrading the technological level of the labor force, and, at the just-concluded National People's Congress, where they presented the 13th Five Year Plan, Prime Minister Li Keqiang used the word "innovation" 61 times in his speech. He said, the aim is to turn China from a trader of quantity to a trader of quality, to basically make it a knowledge-intensive economy.

One of the export flagships of the Chinese is high-speed rail. China has built 125 km of normal railroad, but about 20,000 km of fast train railroads. They want to have 50,000 km by the year 2025, connecting every major city in China with a fast train system.

And I can tell you, I have travelled on fast trains on several occasions in China. These trains go about 310 km/hr, they are very smooth, they don't shake, you don't hear anything. It's an excellent technology and it's one of the export flagships of China.

So this concept of building the One Belt, One Road, which in Asia is also being called the "Asian Connectivity," is very, very attractive. It basically means, it's very high technology. Wu Ji, who is the director of the CAS [Chinese Academy of Sciences] National Space Science Center, just said "space science is inseparable from China's innovation-driven development. If China

High-speed rail is one of the leading exports of China. Premier Li has proposed linking all the capitals of Africa with high-speed rail. Here, bullet trains entering and leaving Shaoguan Station in Shaoguan, China.

youtube/Leonhard Weese

wants to be a strong global nation, it must not only care about its own immediate interests, it must also contribute to humankind. Only in this way can China have real respect in the world."

One can see how advanced the Chinese space program is, for example, by noting that next year the next lunar mission of China will go to the far side of the Moon, which means that landers and rovers will land there, something which has never before been done by mankind. The far side of the Moon will give a new window into space, because, free of the radio-wave noise from the Earth, mankind in a very concrete way can develop a much, much better understanding about what is going on in the nearby universe.

Now, China is doing many, many things right, by simply doing what Germany used to do when Germany was progressing. Shang Fulin, the chairman of the China Banking Regulatory Commission, on a recent occasion said that China will from now on tax monetary speculative transactions with what you would call here a "Tobin tax"; it will promote small and medium-size industries; it will support the savings banks to give credit to these small industries which is what the German *Mittelstand* used to be and it is what made Germany prosperous.

Premier of China's State Council Li Keqiang said

"it is the top priority of the financial sector to support the development of the real economy," as compared, and these are now my words, to the money-printing of Mario Draghi for speculative purposes only.

Now, just two weeks or ten days ago, I just returned from a big conference in New Delhi, the Raisina Dialogue, which is going to be an annual conference organized by the Indian government. I can assure you that there, many speakers from Asian countries, acting foreign ministers, former presidents, leaders of leading institutions, all want to integrate with the One Belt, One Road policy, because they have recognized what the New Silk Road means for countries like Sri Lanka, Bangladesh, Nepal, Bhutan, Afghanistan. It means that they can import the Chinese economic development model and repeat what China did in terms of the very rapid economic development it has undergone in the last 40 years, particularly in the last 25 years.

The Schiller Institute had already proposed some years ago—in 2012—that the *only* way you stop terrorism and stop, now in the last year, the refugee crisis, is by bringing development to Southwest Asia and to Africa. Because only if you have a comprehensive development program for those countries which have been destroyed by wars or a lack of development, as in the case of Africa, only if you apply the method of the New Silk Road to the Middle East, to Africa, can one can solve these problems. This is now on the table.

President Xi Jinping visited Tehran four or five weeks ago, to present the New Silk Road. Shortly after his visit, the first Silk Road train from Yiwu, in China, arrived in Tehran, with, I think, 32 containers. Xi Jinping said that the New Silk Road is a concept to be expanded for the entire Southwest Asian region.

Iranian President Rouhani immediately responded that Iran wants to cooperate. At this conference in

Xi Jinping: Expand the New Silk Road concept to all of Southwest Asia.

New Delhi in which I participated, former Afghan President Karzai said Afghanistan must become the hub of the New Silk Road connecting Asia and Europe, and other leading speakers spoke along the same lines.

I want to emphasize, and you will hear about this from other speakers, I suppose, that the *only* way that we will get out of this crisis, *is* if we develop the Middle East together with Russia, China, India, Iran, Egypt, and other countries of the region, and that we get Germany, France, Italy, the United States, and all other countries to cooperate in what I would call a "Marshall Plan Silk Road perspective for the Middle East and Africa."

I only mention "Marshall Plan," not because it's meant to be a Cold War instrument like the Marshall Plan was, but because it reminds people in Europe that you *can* reconstruct countries which have been destroyed by war, with economic development.

That is the *only* way we can stop the refugee crisis, because only if you give an incentive for people to rebuild their own home countries and you give young people a perspective of hope to become a doctor, a scientist, a teacher, can you dry out terrorism. That is the concrete plan that is now on the table. Either we can get European institutions to go for this alternative, or we will crash against the wall.

Critical Role of Egypt To Bring The New Silk Road to Africa

Here is the edited transcript of Hussein Askary's address to the March 23 EIR *Frankfurt Seminar "Solving the Economic and Refugee Crises with the New Silk Road!" He spoke right after Helga Zepp-LaRouche's keynote address.*

I am a member of the Schiller Institute and *Executive Intelligence Review*, which are organizing this seminar. I came back from Egypt two days ago from a one-week visit there, to launch the Arabic translation of the *EIR* Special Report "The New Silk Road Becomes the World Land-Bridge." I personally, and other people, decided that Egypt should be the place from which to launch the Arabic translation of this massive global development idea, because of the importance of Egypt. Egypt is the most important Arab country, but it's also one of the important countries in Africa.

The idea of the report and joining the Silk Road was actually highly welcomed by the highest levels of the Egyptian government, because they realize now that this is the only solution for the deep economic crisis in Egypt, as well as in the entire region of Southwest Asia, the so-called Middle East, and Africa,

EIRNS/Christopher Lewis

Hussein Askary

by joining forces with China and the BRICS countries to develop their countries internally and utilize the connection to the world economy and the development dynamic which was launched by China with the idea of the New Silk Road.

Helga mentioned the Saudi bombardment of Yemen today. At this moment, there is a similar seminar in the capital of Yemen, in Sana'a, by a group of Yemeni experts and patriots to also launch the Arabic translation. They printed the Arabic version. The seminar is headed by one of the best modern Yemeni poets, Abdulaziz al-Maqaleh. It's organized by our friend, Fouad al-Ghaffari. Right under Saudi bombardment, they established a committee for coordination with the BRICS, and now they are promoting the idea of the New Silk Road and how Yemen will benefit from this.

The World Land-Bridge

These (**Figure 1**) are some of the ideas which I presented in Egypt for people there. The launching was sponsored by the Egyptian Transport Ministry with the presence of the Minister of Transport, Saad el-Geyoushi. But I told

FIGURE 1

The Land-Bridge into the Middle East

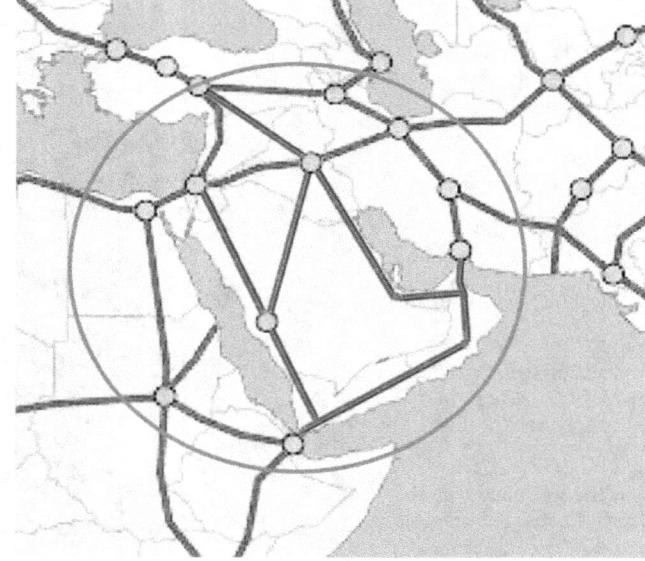

FIGURE 2
LaRouche in Abu Dhabi in 2002

people that our idea is not to build the New Silk Road. We had presented the idea of the New Silk Road 25 years ago, as Helga has said, and China adopted it as its policy.

Our idea is to go from the New Silk Road to the World Land-Bridge, where we connect Africa and the Americas to the Eurasian Land-Bridge. That's the concept. [Shows World Land-Bridge map.] Red lines are where we have a deficit in infrastructure and deficit in development. This is what is missing in the global map, but also a lot is missing in the Americas, even in North America and Europe right now. This is the new concept: It is not simply the New Silk Road, it is the World Land-Bridge. We can unite all nations of the world around one concept of economic development and co-operation.

I had the honor to be in the Schiller Institute and *EIR* in 1996 when the first Eurasian Land-Bridge/New Silk Road was conceived. I worked with Helga and others. I was still a young man. But the idea was a complete transformation. I joined the Schiller Institute in 1994 because I was living in Norway, and the Schiller Institute came to Oslo where Arafat and Rabin and Peres were meeting.

The Schiller Institute people said, "Look, if you don't develop the economy of the Palestinians, the Jordanians, the Lebanese, and the Israelis, there will be no peace." And I immediately joined, because that's the right concept. The usual problem in the Middle East and Africa is that people say the problem is the regime,

and if we get rid of the regime, everything will become good ... and then the economy will solve itself.

But that's a complete lie. However, this is what Europe and the United States are advocating.

People, including in Egypt, now completely understand the idea that the question of the New Silk Road is not trade, it's not moving goods from A to B. The idea is to build development corridors to develop all the areas between A and B. That's the concept. And this idea of a development corridor, all these development corridor lines should be 100-150 km wide, with transport, energy, electricity, oil and gas, water, and building new agricultural and industrial centers.

Mr. Lyndon LaRouche was in Abu Dhabi in 2002, attending a conference about oil and gas. There were four oil ministers in attendance (**Figure 2**). Here, the oil minister of the United Arab Emirates is on the right, next to Mr. LaRouche.

Mr. LaRouche shocked everybody by saying the Gulf countries should gradually stop exporting crude oil. They should use the oil as an industrial material for petrochemicals, chemicals, plastics, and other things, since the value of one barrel of oil transformed into an industrial product would be worth many, many times more than than it would be worth selling it as crude oil, or burning it. And Mr. LaRouche said, "You should utilize your position as a crossroads of the world."

And this is exactly the point which we are trying to promote in Southwest Asia, since this is a unique area. There is no other place on Earth which has the unique characteristics of the region in this zone. It's between three continents. It has more than two-thirds of the world's oil and gas reserves. But more importantly, it has more than 450 million people. Most of them are under the age of 30.

Therefore, they have the whole future in front of them. They also have natural resources. In addition, these are old nations with very, very ancient cultures: Egypt, Ethiopia, Iran, Iraq, Syria. Yemen is also an ancient culture. Although it has not been continuous, as it has in the other cultures I mentioned, the memory of it is still in the Yemen national character.

These are all people who have a very clear idea of their culture and their civilization. In addition, they know that scientific development is the way forward.

But all the advantages of this region have been turned into disadvantages, because it has become the center of global conflict and proxy wars. In this region, we propose—in our Arabic report—the establishment of an Arab Infrastructure Investment Bank with which the nations of the region would be able to develop the region.

In the Gulf countries, not only is there oil, but there is also the sovereign funds of the Gulf countries, amounting to about $2.5-3 trillion in plain hard currency funds.

But it's being used in financial markets, real estate markets in London, in Switzerland, in New York, and similar places. They should instead establish a joint development bank like the Chinese did, establishing the Asian Infrastructure Investment Bank. This region has unique capabilities of being transformed very quickly economically, but the region's nations should utilize the idea of the New Silk Road.

Syria Can Launch a New Policy

Helga referred to the visit by President Xi Jinping in January to Egypt, Iran, and Saudi Arabia. At that moment, Iran and Saudi Arabia were about to enter into a real war, and the Chinese intervened with the idea of the New Silk Road. This was not a warning, but they said, "What the hell are you doing? You are going to destroy the world economy? This is not the way to do things, with crazy religious conflicts. You should work together. We will help you to build your countries, but also help you to work together for development."

This point has been made. Similarly in Egypt: With respect to the idea of the Silk Road, everybody was saying: "Oh, the Silk Road will compete with the Suez Canal traffic," for many, many years. As a result, the New Silk Road was completely blacked out in the Egyptian political and media circles. But now, President Xi Jinping brought the idea of the New Silk Road as actually being beneficial for Egypt, which we can explain quickly.

In the Arabic version of the report, we have the plan for the reconstruction of Syria. As I said, and as Helga said, there will be no peace, there will be no end to terrorism, there will be no end for political oppression, unless we develop this region. And therefore, Syria, ironically, could be the perfect starting place, to establish or put into practice the new economic ideas which we have designed in this report: Utilizing Syria's position as a crossroads with Africa, Europe, and Asia, but also being a nation which is just coming out of war, they actually have no obligation to listen to either the IMF, the World Bank, the EU, the United States, or anybody else!

They can establish their own development bank and issue their own credit. They are not obliged to pay any debt at the moment. This puts Syria in a perfect position to launch a completely new economic policy. And from Syria, you can actually project that idea into many other nations. If one succeeds, many other nations will do it, too.

So, we're not going to go through too many details, because we're short on time. Egypt also could become a model, because Egypt is a very important nation. With President el-Sisi coming to power, Egypt has transformed its identity of itself and what it should do to solve 30 years of accumulation of economic and social problems. But they are in a conflict between doing small solutions here and there, or trying to attain the big change. I think the Egyptian Presidency and leadership—as I have understood it—are going for the big change. Not to solve it with small projects here and there, such as NGOs, EU donations, and other small, limited sources.

Instead, they will focus on mega-projects like the new Suez Canal, which they built in one year instead of eight years. They will build up new agro-industrial zones in the desert, reclaiming the desert of Egypt for demographic expansion. They will use high technology. Now they have an agreement to build nuclear power plants with Russia, which will allow them to start their first nuclear power plant, as well as high-speed railways and similar projects.

They will not start from zero. They will start from the point which China and other nations have attained, and utilize that technology, rather than starting from scratch. As for the idea of internal financing: The new Suez Canal was built by the Egyptian people, who were mobilized by their government to internally raise the money—$8 billion to finish the project in one year. Ethiopia is doing its dam projects in the same way, which is the correct idea: The Millennium Dam and other development projects.

But there is still a conflict over how to proceed with the other projects, whether it will be done by Egyptian financing, or should foreign investment or loans from the IMF and World Bank be sought. There is still a con-

FIGURE 3
Egypt Demographic Map

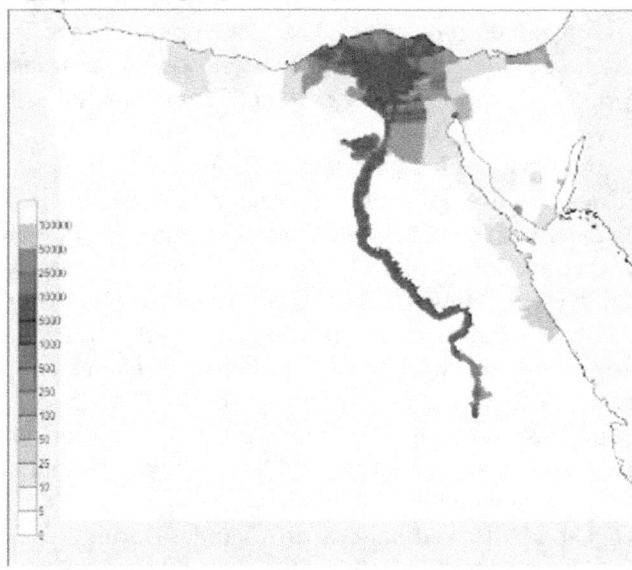

FIGURE 4
Main Projects in Egypt

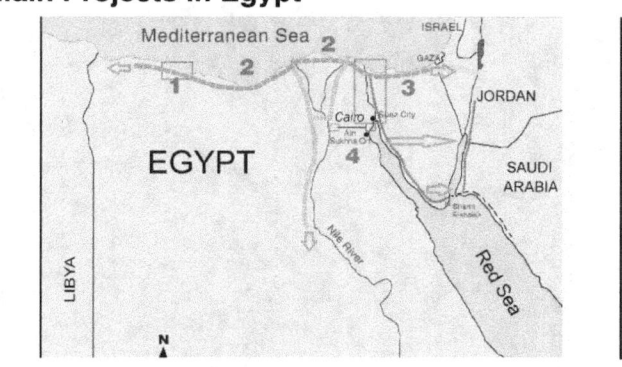

FIGURE 5
Dr. Farouk el-Baz Population Relocation Proposal

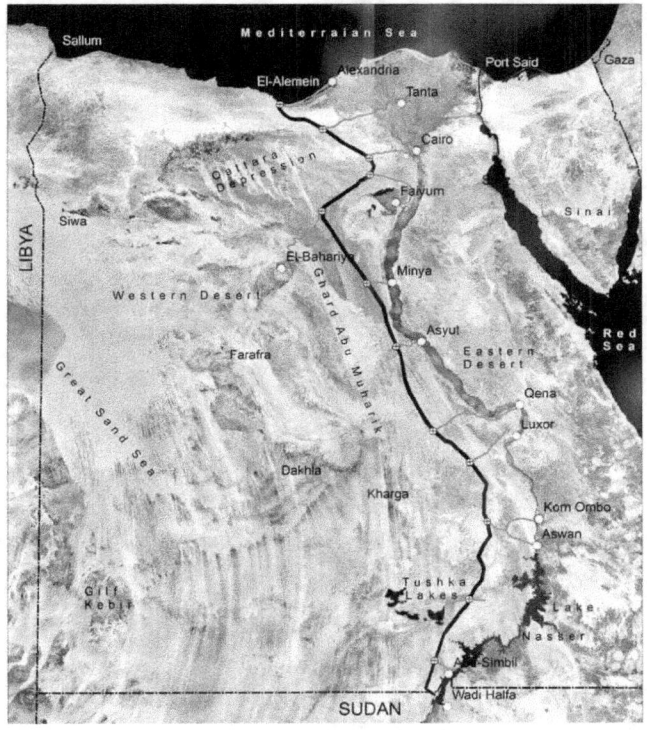

flict inside Egypt as to which way to go, but they have the right overall idea.

And of course, utilizing Egypt's position between Asia, the Arab world, and Africa, is actually now on the agenda, especially after my visit.

This is a disastrous demographic map (**Figure 3**) of Egypt: 90 million people. Ninety-five percent of the people live on only 5% of the land; and 95% of the land is empty. The United States spends billions of dollars to reduce the population of Egypt by various family planning programs, but these donors did not back the idea of opening up new areas for the population to live in!

Instead, they said the solution is to reduce the population of Egypt. And this is what the IMF, the World Bank, the UN, and the United States were providing billions and billions of dollars to do, rather than building new development projects.

Great Projects

But the Egyptians have a different idea. These are some of the main projects they have (**Figure 4**), like the new Suez Canal. In addition, they are building an industrial zone around the Suez Canal and using it as a development corridor for all of the Sinai, but also the eastern part of Egypt, east of Cairo will have new industries. We added to the concept which the Egyptian Transport Minister has now raised, "We're going to do

the extension to Africa: We're going to do the extension to North Africa. And we will have to think now about connecting to the Arabian Peninsula. And also develop the areas on these lines."

This (**Figure 5**) is an idea which has been presented by an Egyptian scientist, Dr. Farouk el-Baz, who worked in NASA, to build a transportation corridor parallel to the Nile and move the concentration of the population from the Nile Valley to the new Nile Valley

FIGURE 6
Cape to Cairo Railroad Proposal

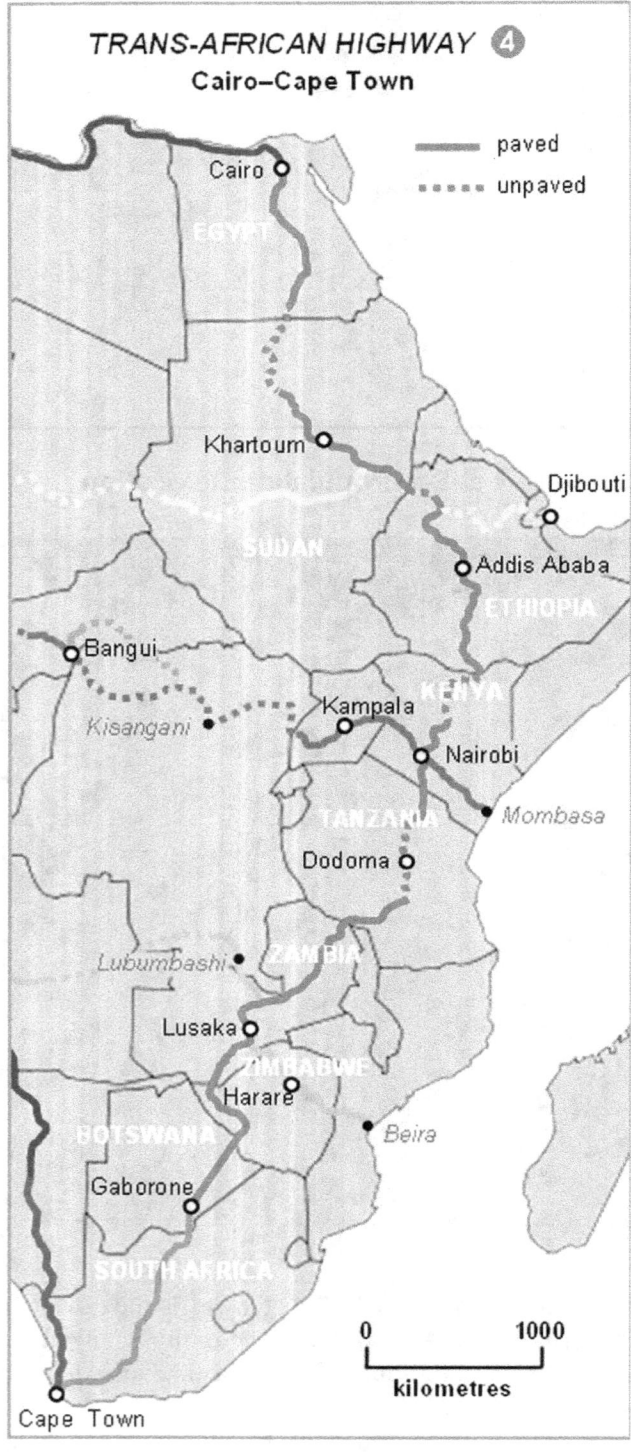

TRANS-AFRICAN HIGHWAY ④
Cairo–Cape Town

— paved
····· unpaved

Cairo
EGYPT

Khartoum
Djibouti
SUDAN
Addis Ababa
ETHIOPIA
Bangui
Kampala
Kisangani
KENYA
Nairobi
TANZANIA
Mombasa
Dodoma
Lubumbashi
ZAMBIA
Lusaka
ZIMBABWE
Harare
Beira
BOTSWANA
Gaborone
SOUTH AFRICA
Cape Town

0   1000
kilometres

by building railroads and roads and connecting them to the major cities. I added the green zones where the Egyptian government is intending to reclaim four mil-lion hectares of land to give for settlement to young people and companies. The government builds houses for them, builds the infrastructure, and gives them a loan for the first three years so they can grow food and set up small industries. The development corridor should be a bit further into the desert, so you can transform the demographics and economic situation in Egypt.

And then comes the idea of connecting Egypt to Africa (**Figure 6**). There are projects which have been on the drawing board since the 1970s in the Lagos Plan of Action, for example. But nobody did anything to build them. Now the Egyptian government and the South African government are intending to do that, from south and north to support the idea of connecting all of East Africa from north to south: The Cairo to Cape Town Railway. This is now actively being considered. It intersects Sudan, Ethiopia, Kenya, Tanzania, Zambia, Zimbabwe, and South Africa.

The landlocked nations of Rwanda, Burundi eastern Democratic Republic of Congo, and South Sudan which have never had rail access to the sea, will be able to access South Africa and Egypt by building connections to the Cape to Cairo trunk line. The three nations will also be able to eventually access the standard-gauge railway being built by China from the port city of Mombasa, to Nairobi and then to Kampala, Uganda.

Then the Nile River and the other rivers in Africa could be connected together (**Figure 7**) to have a river transport corridor from the north to the south, in the same way that the Rhine-Main-Danube are connected now, which provides transportation from East Europe and Western Europe. Here, the concept is the same.

We have our friend, Aiman Rsheed, an engineer in Egypt, who has developed the concept of building the Africa Pass he calls it (**Figure 8**), which goes close to the Libyan border. It is all desert today, but there are enormous water resources accessible there, there is fertile land, and there is no reason why that part of Egypt is not being developed.

There is also a possible east-west connection from either Port Sudan in Sudan, or Djibouti, to Dakar in Senegal, to connect the entire Sahel region with modern infrastructure. This idea is supported by the Organization of the Islamic Conference, but no financing has been forwarded to it.

This is the point at which China comes into the picture, and transforms the situation. The Chinese say, okay, this is an enormous economic development

FIGURE 7
Proposal to Link African Rivers

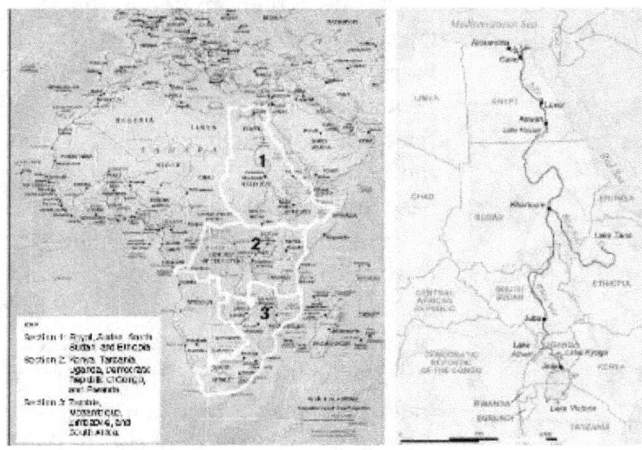

potential, and it's rich with raw materials. It has also large populations, agriculture, every requirement you need to develop that region, but it lacks infrastructure.

The Chinese have offered to build these transport corridors from the ports in Mombasa and Lamu in Kenya, on the Indian Ocean, and open up all these landlocked countries, such as Ethiopia, South Sudan, and the Central African Great Lakes region, including eastern Democratic Republic of Congo, Uganda, Rwanda, and Burundi.

Such areas or nations need the rail infrastructure for both exports and imports of goods and technology, to open up that whole region for development.

These nations only need to develop infrastructure and educate the labor force. The Chinese are training Ugandan Army personnel to turn them into an Army Corps of Engineers, enabling them to participate in building railroads and developing the country instead of policing the population!

Another undertaking is the Trans-Aqua project, which was thought up by Dr. Vichi. But this is the kind of concept I was presenting in Egypt, to emphasize that the time of mega-projects is back. The Chinese have proven it. These massive major infrastructure and development projects can be built. They have been undermined by the trans-Atlantic financial world, which claims that these mega-projects are romantic ideas. If a military dictator wants to become famous in history, he will build a huge football stadium and call it "President So-and-So" Stadium. But project opponents pretend the same is true of these mega-projects. However,

FIGURE 8
Africa Pass

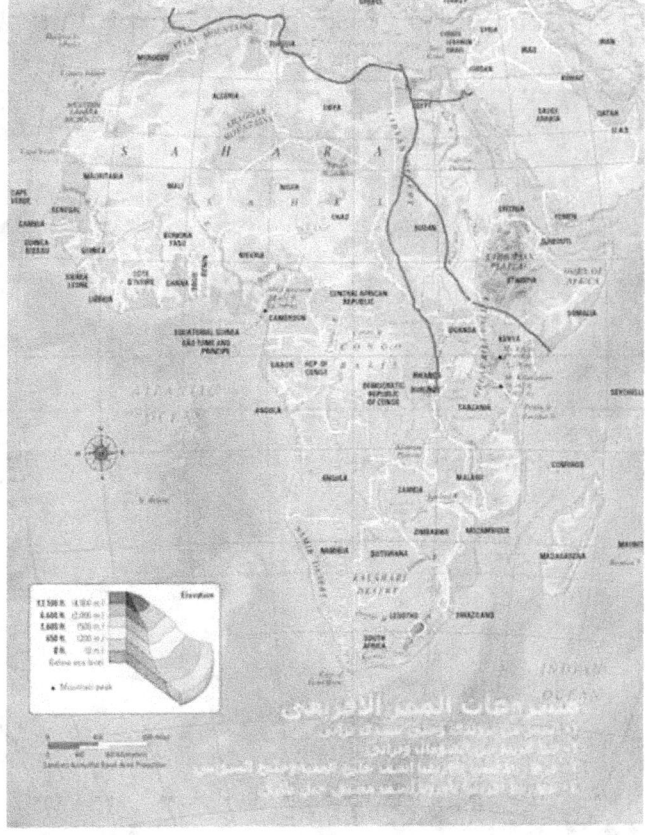

mega-projects are now back on the map, and all they have potential to be implemented. This is the idea of saving Lake Chad.

Africa could then be transformed from the colonial system to the modern sovereign, community of sovereign nations system.

The Right Way for Egypt

The Transportation Minister of Egypt, Dr. Saad El-Geyoushi (**Figure 9**). He said "I have to present this report to the Egyptian people." But he also announced for the first time in this press conference, that Egypt is intending to invest 1 trillion Egyptian pounds, which is about $100 billion, over the next 14 years, on roads, railways, and logistics centers. He also announced that Egypt is negotiating with other nations in Africa to build a 50,000 km network of roads and railways. This was information coming out for the first time. But he said, "Our intention is to integrate Egypt's vision," we have a plan for 2030, "we will integrate our internal develop-

FIGURE 9
Egypt Transportation Minister Dr. Saad El-Geyoushi

FIGURE 10
Admiral Mohab Mamish

FIGURE 11
Former Egyptian Prime Minister Essam Sharaf

ment with the idea of the New Silk Road." So, there are clear intentions.

We were then invited to the Suez Canal Authority (**Figure 10**). This is Adm. Mohab Mamish, a military general in the navy. He's a close friend of President el-Sisi. He was the general who made sure that the new Suez Canal was dug in just one year, as the President had ordered, to prove to the world that Egyptians can do these massive projects. They can raise the money for them, they can build them. Of course, they got technical help from other countries, but the concept is that Egypt can do these things, with support.

We were also taken on a boat trip in the new Suez Canal. but the point was that they welcomed the Land-Bridge development corridor idea very, very much. It's not the first time they have heard about it, but it's the first time they have heard, and seen a concept which they themselves had in their minds, but that they never believed could become a reality on a global scale.

When we presented the idea of the New Silk Road, what the Chinese are doing, what the BRICS nations are doing, and what the Egyptians themselves can do, then the whole situation becomes transformed. We had four or five seminars. We had seminars every day—televised events. But the gentleman there (**Figure 11**) is the former Prime Minister of Egypt, Essam Sharaf, he responded: "I was just in China, and I'm very, very happy to see this idea here in Egypt." He was surprised, and he said, "This is the right way for Egypt to go. We have to study this and implement this, because for 30 years we have not done enough for the development of Egypt."

We also had other seminars. Thank you very much.

Transaqua: How to Develop The Sahel and Central Africa

The Transaqua proposal—for the transfer of water from the Congo River basin to dying Lake Chad—is an exemplar of the Silk Road approach to developing the Sahel and Central Africa. Governments in the region are now prepared to undertake a feasibility study. The Transaqua project was a major subject of the March 23 Frankfurt conference on "Solving the Economic and Refugee Crises through the New Silk Road." Dr. Marcello Vichi, author of the Transaqua concept, reviewed the history of the idea. His colleague, engineer Andrea Mangano, presented the parameters of the problem and the specifics of the plan. Mohammed Bila of the Lake Chad Basin Commission (LCBC) described the social and economic consequences of decades of inaction, establishing the necessity to act now. Edited excerpts from these presentations follow.

Vichi: Transaqua—From Dream to Reality?

After 35 years that I have been writing and talking about Lake Chad—about how to avoid its progressive drying, about the best means to combat the ever more evident desertification, a tragedy for the survival of millions of people depending on what used to be the fourth sweet-water lake in Africa—after having listened to reams of useless commentaries and dozens of beautiful articles about the argument, here, today I feel rather satisfied.

In fact, I have recently "passed the baton." After 35 years of general indifference, in these last months there has been an official statement of conscience: The interested African countries have decided to determine the technical feasibility of "Transaqua—an Idea for the Sahel."

The next speaker, my colleague Eng. Andrea Mangano, will illustrate the Transaqua idea in detail. I will limit myself to some of the most significant aspects of the history of the idea.

Schiller Institute

Dr. Marcello Vichi, author of the Transaqua concept: After writing and talking about how to bring Lake Chad back to life for 35 years, I have passed the baton: The interested African governments have decided to study its technical feasibility. Here, Vichi speaks at a 2011 Schiller Institute event.

Between 1982 and 1985, Bonifica, a consulting engineering firm belonging to the IRI group in Italy, published three technical-promotional documents in three languages.

The then chairman of IRI and I presented Transaqua at the Rio de Janeiro Earth Summit in 1992.

In 1988, a popular scientific program of RAI Italian national television effectively illustrated the Transaqua idea, hosting Bukar Shaib, then chairman of the LCBC. On that occasion, Mr. Shaib characterized as "catastrophic" the condition of the lake. Lake Chad, he said, "constitutes a barrier to the spread of the desert" which, in the absence of initiatives,

In 1988, Dr. Bukar Shaib said that the only solution for the "catastrophic" condition of Lake Chad was the transfer of water from tributaries of the River Congo to the Chad basin. Shaib—Nigeria's Minister of Agriculture and Chairman of the Lake Chad Basin Commission for much of the 1980s—spoke on Italian national television.

UN Food and Agriculture Organization

"will cross the Sahel zone and reach Central Africa." During that same television interview, Mr. Shaib made it clear that he considered the project of water transfer from the Congo basin to the Chad basin as the only one possible and reported that he had solicited an engagement by United Nations Environment Programme during a summit of the leaders of the four countries that share the lake shore in April 1984. He thanked Bonifica for having developed the idea of Transaqua on its own initiative ("we haven't asked anything of Bonifica," he said), declaring also that there was the political will to save "from 10 to 20 million people that didn't intend to become refugees," and concluded: "We political leaders cannot cross our arms and sit down."

The member countries of the LCBC did not show in that period the same interest in the Transaqua idea. Perhaps they considered it excessively ambitious, megalomaniac, or utopian, and therefore unfeasible—an opinion largely shared, then and now, by many international agencies.

'Let Us Help Them at Home'

Today, distressed by what is considered an invasion of desperate populations of truly biblical proportions, with no hope for work and survival, many European politicians have discovered a new approach: *"Let us help them at their home."* Better late than never! The "megalomania" of which Transaqua has always been accused, could be simply considered today the right approach to deal with the enormous problems of the African continent (and of the consequences that result, and even more will result ... at *"our home"*)!

An Idea whose technical feasibility the member countries of the LCBC seem to intend to check now. It looks like they intend to see whether Transaqua could really become a second Nile in the heart of Africa, able to definitely solve the problem of Lake Chad.

What should be done is nothing else than transferring an enormous quantity of water from the catchment basin of the Congo River to the basin of Lake Chad. And there are no alternatives to this hypothesis. And the hypothesis can't be to transfer a few hundreds of cubic meters per second, but at least 1,500 to 2,000 m^3 per second. And it isn't even possible to consider the hypothesis to pump water into the lake as realistic, not only because equipment of this magnitude and power are unprecedented in the world, but essentially because the issue is revitalizing, and thus keeping the water level, of a real sea, which you cannot expect to achieve by pumping—an idea that, besides being "pharaonic," would also be stupid.

The decision today is just a political one. Concerned African countries, and only they, will be able to decide whether to leave the lake and the people living around it to its natural destiny, or to determine the feasibility of Transaqua. If such a study were to confirm the feasibility of the idea, the consequent political decisions would be much more engaging, because they would initiate a real and effective African renaissance.

Our hope is that any kind of solution today—after thirty and more years of guilty inactivity—is not entrusted only to arms and to more and more endemic warfare, nourished by the desperation of new generations. The great construction yard and the massive investments that, in the course of a few decades, could directly and indirectly engage the labor force of a dozen countries in Central Africa, would be able to employ tremendous local human resources for several generations of Africans. These massive investments could direct current flows of migrants towards an enormous developing area that, from being a land of hunger and famine, could gradually transform itself into a series of large work sites producing wealth.

Mangano: The Plan Itself

About 30 million people currently live in the watershed of Lake Chad, now only a tenth of its size in 1973. The lake is situated in the Sahel region where Niger,

FIGURE 1

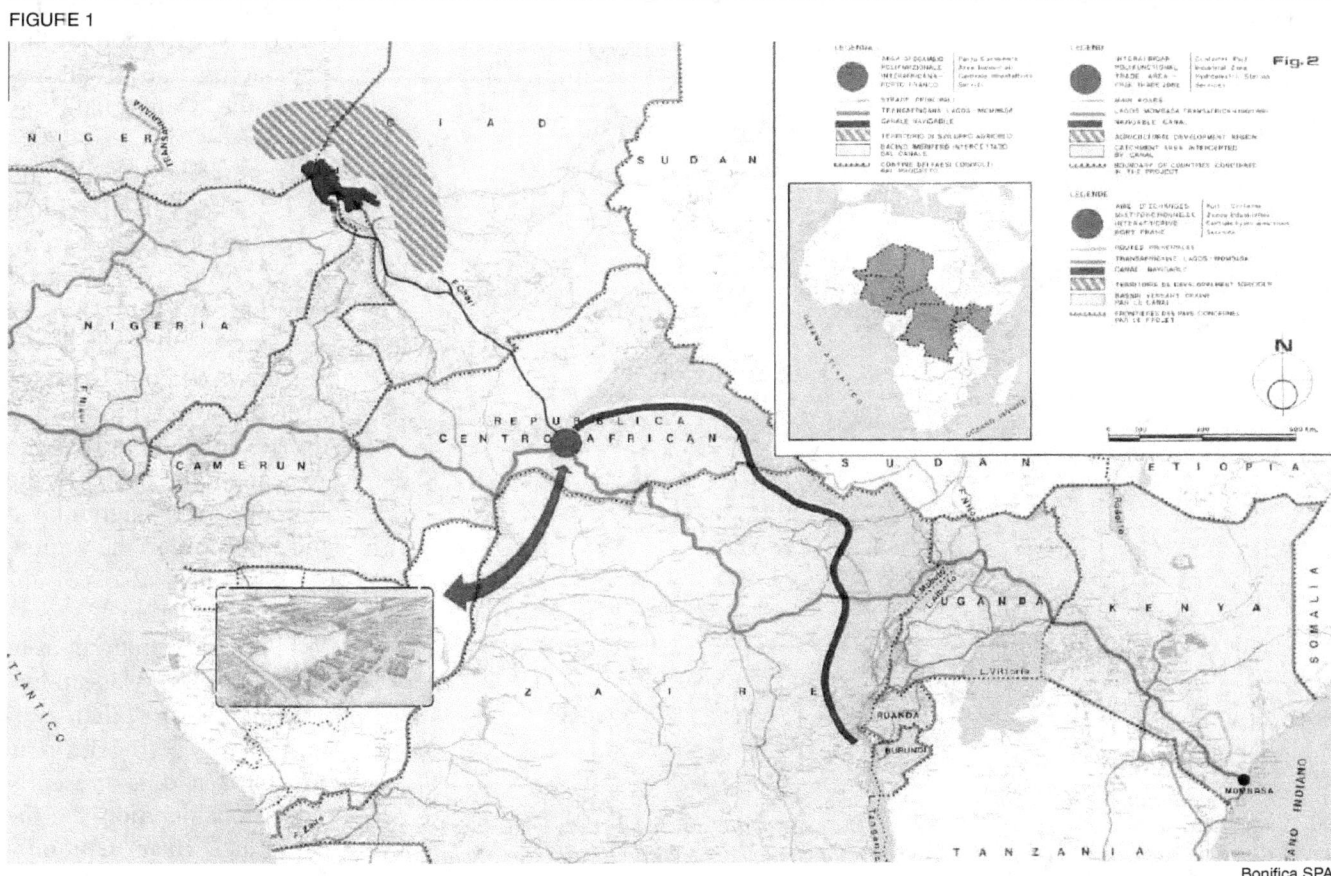

Bonifica SPA

The blue ribbon is the canal that captures some of the water from the upper reaches of the Congo River tributaries in the yellow catchment area. (The Congo River system itself is a background feature in pale blue, identified at its mouth as F. Zaire. The Democratic Republic of Congo and the Congo River were both known as Zaire during the rule of President Mobutu Sese Seko.) The canal then feeds the water across the divide between the Congo and Chari basins and into the Chari River at the red spot; the Chari empties into Lake Chad. The red spot also signifies a proposed inland container port, industrial zone, and hydroelectric station. The green hatched area next to Lake Chad is an agricultural development region. The red ribbon is the projected route of a Lagos-Mombasa Transafrican Highway, which runs close to the inland container port.

Chad, Nigeria, and Cameroon meet. Its watershed covers an area larger than that of Nigeria and Chad combined (approximately 2.4 million km²).

The size of the lake has always varied greatly due to natural climatic fluctuations. But the massive shrinking of its surface area that began in 1973, is not only because of the great decrease in rainfall, but also because the population has increased, resulting in greater water consumption, mainly for irrigation. The surface area of 25,000 km² in 1973 had become 2,500 km² in 2015, while the watershed population of 8 million in 1973 had grown to 30 million in 2015.

Annual average rainfall within the lake's basin varies between almost zero in the northern desert and more than 700 millimeters in the southern part, and has decreased by about 15% in the last 20 years.

Lake Chad is—or at least was—one of the largest endorheic lakes in the world and the largest in Africa. These are the lakes that are not way stations on river systems that flow into the sea; rather, they have no outlet and lose water only by evaporation and infiltration. Other examples are the Dead Sea, Lake Turkana (Kenya), and Lake Urmia (Iran). An endorheic basin has a very unstable equilibrium—there is no guarantee of maintaining a certain level thanks to surplus water flowing to the sea. If water is taken for use upstream, the lake cannot but shrink.

When water is short in a given place, either you

FIGURE 2

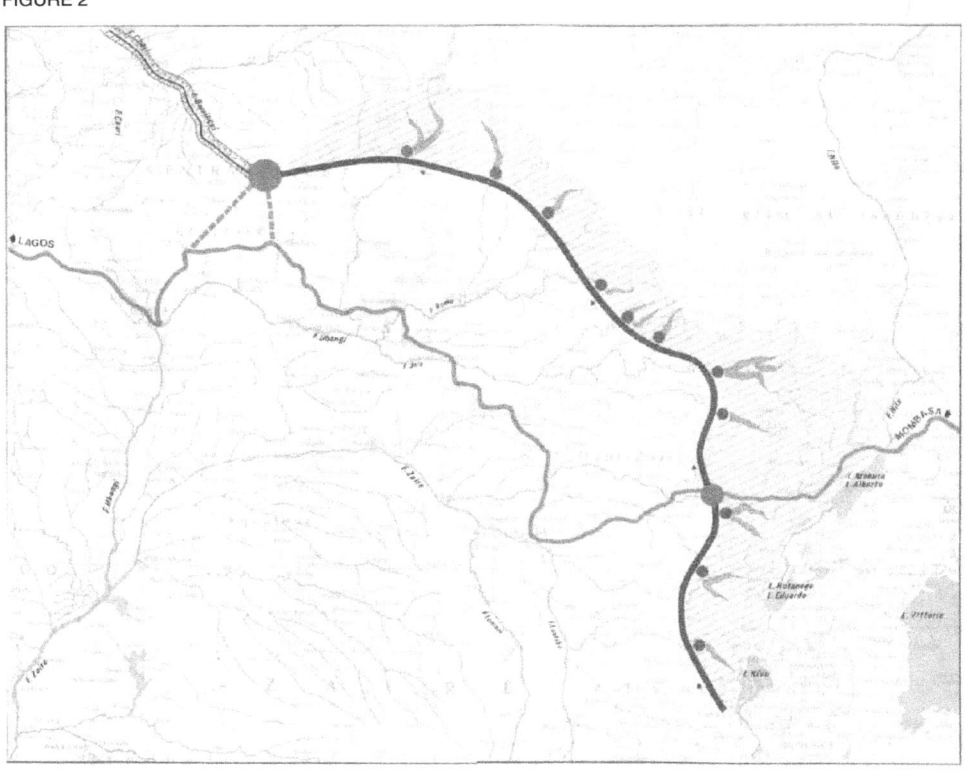

Bonifica SPA

The canal will be a development corridor. The darker red dots are river ports and the green area upstream from each is an agricultural development area. The canal will have a road alongside and may itself be navigable.

upstream tributaries of the Congo River and convey this water across the divide between the Congo and the Chari basins.

The diverted flow would reach Lake Chad through one of the Chari River tributaries, properly reshaped (see **Figures 1 and 2**). In its fall toward Lake Chad, the diverted flow could be used for hydropower production. A road should be built along the canal to become the backbone of international land transport in the region. The canal may also be suitable for navigation.

This idea, stemming from the early 1920s, was studied by Bonifica, an Italian consulting engineering firm, in the 1980s and is presently under consideration by the Lake Chad Basin Commission.

bring the water in, or people will migrate elsewhere.

The Transaqua Idea

The Transaqua solution is to bring water from the Congo River basin to the thirsty Chad region and to increase irrigated agriculture, restore the lake, produce hydropower, and improve
international transport in the region.

The immense Congo River basin is lightly populated and discharges into the Atlantic Ocean an average of 40,000 m³ per second, equivalent to 1.25 trillion m³ per year, or 14 times the discharge of the Rhine at its mouth. How much of this amount could possibly be diverted into the Chad basin has to be studied.

A very preliminary estimate indicates that up to 100 billion m³ per year could be diverted, less than 8% of the Congo discharge, but enough to ensure the restoration of Lake Chad and irrigation of up to 3 million hectares (7.4 million acres).

A canal would intercept part of the discharges of the

Bila: The Consequences of Inaction

It is actually uplifting for me to meet you. The reason is that I never knew about the Silk Road until today, and this is an idea that has been under development for the last 25 years. Equally, we talk about projects, and an idea that another missionary, Dr. Marcello Vichi, had 35 years ago. But now, at the Lake Chad Basin Commission, we look at this idea as the solution to our problems.

Lake Chad as a problem started in 1973. That was when the droughts in the area began. This drought led to a 40% decrease in the rainfall in the Sahel region. The impact on Lake Chad is that there is 40% reduction of the inflow into the lake.

The immediate effect of that drought was that a massive number of people in the Sahel, the region to the south of the Sahara, moved further south. It used to have about 200 to 300 millimeters of rainfall annually, so that level of rainfall was not there any more. The immediate impact was that by 1975, a lot of people went to the south, from Niger, from Mali, people moved south, because they could no longer survive there.

Later on there was an improvement in the amount of rainfall, but this southward movement did not stop. This is natural. If you move from a place where there is a drought, you don't want to move back where there is no drought. So this movement has continued for the past 25 years. And nobody has been talking about it.

The effect is what we are seeing now: The cattle raisers lost a lot of their cattle because of the drought. So it is natural for them to move south where there is more rainfall. And they are gradually moving. It is not a movement that somebody is directing. People start moving to where they have grass and grazing room for their cattle.

But the people who they are encountering have a different religion. And their economy is different: They are farmers, not pastoralists.

That is the basis for the problems in the Lake Chad basin. It started in Chad and Mali, and it is still going on in Darfur. It moved down into the north of Nigeria—this is the Boko Haram area—and it moved south into the Central African Republic. This is where you have farmers with agricultural areas. The migrants are not from this region, they are not from this country, and they started moving in.

What you get in the news is that Christian nations are fighting Muslims. But the real issue is that people have been losing their cattle, so they are moving south.

So that is the reality, and it is still happening, even within Nigeria. In the middle part of Nigeria, just about a month ago, thousands of people in a village were killed. This is the problem that we are facing.

Now why did we decide to look into Transaqua? Because Dr. Marcello Vichi, 35 years ago, predicted this

EIRNS/Christopher Lewis

Mohammed Bila of the Lake Chad Basin Commission: "What everybody said was: 'The Transaqua idea is too big; we know no one who will do it.'" But now, facing the consequences of decades of inaction, "we have to look at this proposal: Is it feasible? And that is where we are right now."

thing would happen.

What everybody always said was: The Transaqua idea is too big, we know no one to do it. This is a big project for Africa. But over those 35 years, how much development has it brought to Africa to try to help refugees, to try to support the local farmers, to try to support local people? If instead we had invested in this, we might not have these problems today.

So this led us to the decision that we have to look at this proposal: Is it feasible? And that is where we are right now.

On the Industrialization of Africa

For many years, *EIR* and the Schiller Institutes have addressed the industrialization of Africa, including the problem of the desertification of the Sahel and the drying up of Lake Chad. Some of the resulting publications follow.

How the International Development Bank Will Work: IDB, by Lyndon H. LaRouche, 1975.

The Industrialization of Africa, by the Fusion Energy Foundation, Wiesbaden, 1980.

"The Congo-Chad Water Transfer: The Main Features of a Feasibility Study," by Marcello Vichi, 2010.

"Transaqua Development for Africa," an address by Marcello Vichi, 2011.

"Lake Chad, Transaqua Basis for New Africa," by Lawrence Freeman, *EIR*, Dec. 5, 2014.

The New Silk Road Becomes The World Land-Bridge, *EIR* Special Report, 2014, "Part 10. Africa—Test of Global Progress."

What Kind of Development Plan Can Stop the Global Crisis?

Claudio Celani, who moderated the March 23 seminar in Frankfurt, Germany, asked Helga Zepp-LaRouche the first question during the dialogue period.

Claudio Celani: What is the difference between your idea of the Marshall Plan—"Marshall Plan for the Middle East," and what the German government is proposing, because the German government also came out talking about a Marshall Plan?

Helga Zepp-LaRouche: I think it is important to recognize that there is such a thing as the British Empire. Now people somehow have the illusion that the British Empire vanished with the end of the Second World War, but the reality is that the only reason why Africa, for example, is in the condition it is in right now, and why Southwest Asia is facing this refugee crisis, is because there are people who think there are too many people in the world, and who are creating conditions for depopulation. Look at Prince Philip: Prince Philip has said many times that he wants to be reincarnated as a virus, in order to contribute more to reducing the world population.

Look at the whole paradigm shift which occurred beginning approximately 50 years ago, when the Club of Rome started to come out with the propaganda about limited resources, the *Limits to Growth* book. This is a lie! There are no limits to growth! What a resource is, is entirely defined by the level of technology with which you look at this resource. Look at who blocked dams, projects, the Lake Chad project, and many other projects: the World Wildlife Fund and other green organizations.

I think in Ethiopia you have had the experience that very valid projects were blocked. Lake Chad: Why is the project blocked? Because there are some greenies who think that it's important to save a little louse, or a fly, or a spider, more so than hundreds of millions of human beings!

Despite the problems with the German government—I'm known not to be a fan of Mrs. Merkel, which I have have made clear many times—but when she said, "OK, we can do it, we can take these refugees," this was the first time, I said, "OK, she's doing the right thing."

But what is happening now is really disgusting and has to be changed! Because as the gentleman before was saying, to bet on the Turkish government to solve the refugee crisis is disgusting, it is genocidal, it is absolutely something we have to change [applause], because the German government is pragmatic. And it's very diplomatic of me to say that. But it is wavering between being a poodle for London and Washington, and for the first time taking baby steps in the right direction. But they did not have the clarity to think it through.

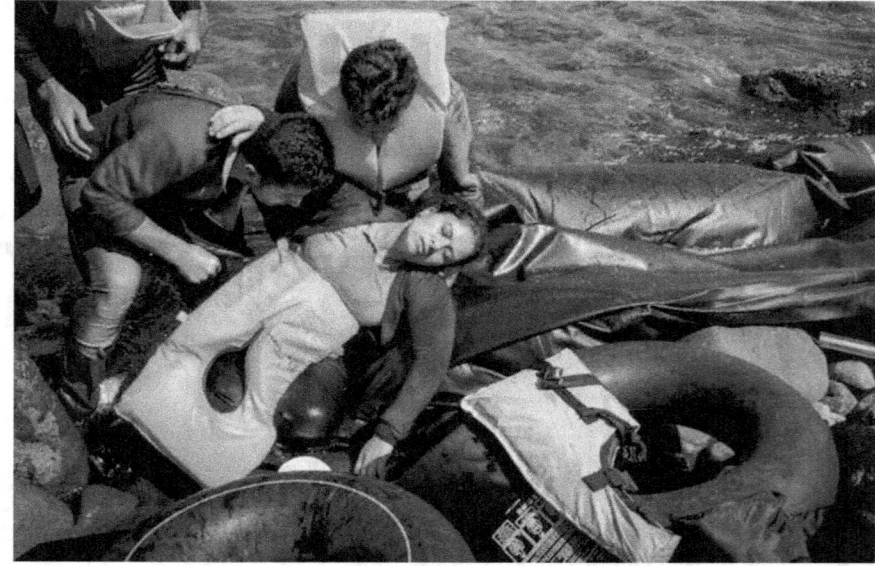

UNHCR/I. Prickett

One of countless refugees from Syria. This woman had collapsed from seasickness and fatigue after the journey from Turkey to the island of Lesbos.

Because if you think in small steps, and it is known that Mrs. Merkel thinks in small steps, forget it! We are in an *epochal* crisis! We are in a crisis of civilization! Everything is breaking down that people believed would be safe such as pensions and education.

Consider the United States, which is in a breakdown crisis beyond belief! Why do you think you have all these shootings in the schools? Why do you think there is a heroin epidemic in the United States, which has increased the suicide rate by four times since Bush Junior became President, continued by the Obama Administration? The United States is in a classical breakdown crisis, and Europe is in the same condition!

So, the situation really requires a paradigm shift. I mean, look, even Schäuble, who is responsible for the collapse of the Greek economy by one-third, who is responsible for the misery of the people of Southern Europe, is now talking about a "Marshall Plan." Can we trust him?

No! Because the German government is completely green. It left nuclear energy for no good reason. I'm being asked all the time, in the U.S. Congress or in other countries where I talk to people, "The Germans must have some solution to fusion power. They cannot be so stupid as to exit nuclear energy without having an alternative."

So, I think we have to recognize that we're dealing with a Satanic force! A force which is right now dominating the world in the form of the British Empire, which is just another word for the central banks, the investment funds, the hedge funds, and the financial institutions, who are now *at the end of their rope.* If you go for hyper-inflationary helicopter money, then that's the end!

So we have to have a complete break in the situation and we have to change. Because if you continue on this road, civilization may not make it! Because with the collapse of the financial system, you have also the war danger: We haven't talked about this very much today because we have to talk about the solution, but we are right now closer to World War III than we were at the height of the Cold War, and that is not just what we say. That has been said by Helmut Schmidt, by Gorbachov, by Ted Postol, by many other nuclear experts, who are closely studying the fact that the two nuclear powers are on launch-on-warning all the time.

Either side only has five minutes to make a decision to launch, once it is alerted that the other side has launched a missile. *Five minutes—five minutes!* We are sitting on a volcano of the financial collapse of the entire trans-Atlantic sector, we're sitting on the volcano of a potential thermonuclear war, which if it happened, would lead to the annihilation of humankind: That's where we are!

Therefore, what we are proposing is not anything like what the German government is proposing; or, the EU, even less so. The EU is a force for disaster and should be abandoned as quickly as possible.

Why do you think these development projects have not been realized? They have invented a terminology—"appropriate technology," which means no technology; "sustainable development" which means starve to death, depopulate. All of these things must be debunked as frauds! They don't want Africa to develop! They don't want the Middle East to develop! They think population reduction is a good thing!

Schellnhuber, who is a charlatan, who is an advisor to Merkel, has said explicitly they want to have the world population at 1 billion people. And he has been unfortunately able to subvert the Vatican, to sneak the fraud that climate change is the result of CO_2 into the new Encyclical of the Pope and have the Pope endorse this fraud, which is not true!

Climate change is taking place, but climate change has something to do with the position of the Solar system in the Galaxy, with eruptions on the Sun, with things which have been studied for a very long time. And if you believe the idea that CO_2 emissions cause climate change, you can believe the Easter bunny lays eggs! You know, I discovered at the age of four that this was a lie. [laughter] I found my uncle hiding eggs so that I could find them later.

I just want to say this is a much more serious problem, and we have to start to understand that this is the fate of civilization which at stake.

So what we are proposing with the World Land-bridge—maybe you can see the back side of the program—we are talking about a rebuilding of the entire world economy. We want to have development of all the continents, and do it in the same way that all industrial revolutions *always* took place—in Germany, in Russia, in the United States: You start with infrastructure. Because without infrastructure you can't even have agriculture. Look at India, for example: 38% of the food produced is rotting because of a lack of food processing and a lack of infrastructure. A country like South Sudan has about the richest soil in the world, and you could have three to four harvests a year, but you need infrastructure to transport it.

So either we become rational, and develop this planet of ours as *one humanity*, and replace geopolitics, and instead start with the common aims of mankind,—and that is what we have to do!

So it would be very easy: We started to evolve an African development plan in the 1970s! In 1980, we published the first book about African development. It could be done. We could eliminate hunger in Africa in half a year. We could have an end to poverty in five years. We could have a decent living standard in 10-20 years from now.

What is lacking is the political will. And I tell you this: This refugee crisis will become the game-changer, or we will not make it. Because the fact that this Turkey deal will not work, will become more apparent by the day. It's already not working. And we have to create a mass movement for development in Europe, and we have to join hands with people in Africa, in Asia, and in other continents, to turn this situation around. And I'm very optimistic that it can be done, because if you only look at the situation from an internal German perspective, it looks horrible, because the Germans have become stupid, they have become arrogant, and they think they know everything, and in reality they know very little. And they have their nose stuck high in the air while they understand almost nothing.

But, fortunately, that is not the only perspective you can see the world from. China right now has put an alternative on the table in the form of the Silk Road and the "win-win" perspective. The efforts of the BRICS countries have not been eliminated, as some people would like, although the efforts to carry out regime change in South Africa and Brazil are very active. But right now, the winning model *is* the New Silk Road, and we have to just make sure that the people in Europe know about this alternative, and we have to start fighting for the realization of these issues because it is our own interest that this one planet which we have, survives!

And I can only propose that we really use this seminar, not just to listen to presentations, but to start to fight for implementation of these ideas, and to give hell to your parliamentarian, your mayor, and your city council! Call them up and say, "You are responsible for what happens." You have to develop citizens' fighting spirits. People are like lambs going to the slaughter. And I want to arouse your passion to save civilization, because that is what is as at stake!

EIR Seminar Open Discussion

Here are excerpts of the discussion period which followed the presentations at the March 23, 2016 EIR *seminar in Frankfurt, Germany.*

Question: [BüSo organizer] I would like to ask Hussein a question, because about two years ago the Egyptian ambassador gave a presentation in Berlin, in which he gave a certain insight into the country, how it works, the role of the military, certain things that were quite interesting.

Now, your visit in Egypt and that really successful trip presenting this report came as a big surprise to me; I was not prepared, but I was very happy to hear about it. My question is this: Knowing very little about the general region, I would like to know, —I work in Berlin; obviously, we have some people we can approach immediately, not just with the report, but also the fact that this took place. But I don't know much about the relations of Egypt to neighboring countries—or I don't know, Israel—but the larger region. I would like to ask you for some hints or certain guidelines on how to approach this. Or maybe there are also other countries or other organizations that would be a natural target to approach in Berlin? Thank you.

A New World Being Shaped

Hussein Askary: There's one thing, it's connected to our friend, Camille about Syria, the enormous and horrendous suffering that the Syrian people have to go through because of global politics and international politics. But the whole issue of our work and this report and everything we are doing and Helga is doing, is that we are trying to show, on a realistic basis that a new dynamic is taking place in the world. There is a new world order being shaped, although it's not so dominant in the West, but it's making itself felt in many parts of the world: Through the work of the BRICS nations, through the Chinese New Silk Road, and everything Helga has said. And it's being felt all around the world. People are looking forward to it.

But there is another aspect, because, we have discussed, we have written all about who is behind the destruction of the Middle East and Libya and all these forces. What we have to do now is to look into the

EIRNS/Christopher Lewis

The conference panel (from left): Hussein Askary, Consul General Mehreteab Mulugeta Haile, Claudio Celani, Helga Zepp-LaRouche, Marcello Vichi, and Andrea Mangano (speaking).

future, and see what is the dynamic that is needed to reverse this situation. And we are not talking about dreams or anything, because about 25 years ago, this whole New Silk Road thing was something like a dream, *but* there was a force, there was another work behind it, which Helga personally took on her own, but China, a major power, put all its force behind it.

Now, something else is going on in Syria, in other words the Russian President, who has proven that he is a real strategic genius, has intervened to change the whole picture through the intervention in Syria. So we either have World War III or the whole world order should change. That's what was at stake, when the Russian Prime Minister in the Munich [Security] Conference said, we are on the verge of World War III, he was not trying to bluff the others to surrender, he was not trying to scare people. This was a very, very realistic statement.

But what the Russians are trying to do is say, OK, we have two cops: The Chinese are coming with the soft power, saying we can help you build your country, build your region. If you don't accept our solution, you can get the Russian treatment, you know. That's what ISIS got in Syria. ISIS is going to disappear in Syria, they will disappear in Iraq, soon. And I'm very sure of that.

The problem is that policies that created ISIS are not being changed. The source of ISIS, the regime change policies in the West, are still—I mean, people are not being taken for trial in Brussels, NATO chiefs or people in the United States who supported this whole invasion of Libya, who supported the invasion of Iraq, I don't see them being on trial right now. So there's a lot of work to be done.

But the Russians and the Chinese specifically say that there's a new strategy we can work on. Do you want to fight terrorism, you fight terrorism with us. You want to build your economy, you build your economy with us. The Western, the trans-Atlantic model has *failed.* You just look at the world, and you can see, it has failed miserably. So there's a new situation in the world, and you have to utilize that.

And this was my message also in Egypt. Egypt is— Ministers and other people would say, "the situation here is very, very, very bad." I mean, they say it themselves, "we have a horrible situation." Egypt is under attack by terrorists; the Egyptian currency is under attack, it has been collapsing, and the central bank has been using the same IMF model by buying dollars in the market and they drained all their reserves by trying to strengthen the currency, rather than stopping the currency speculation. And there are many outside forces who are trying to destroy the Egyptian currency. The level of unemployment, many of these things are still here, because you have an accumulation of 30 years of

---

The Russians and Chinese say there is a new strategy we can work on. Do you want to fight terrorism, you fight terrorism with us. You want to build your economy, you build your economy with us. The Western trans-Atlantic model has failed.

---

the destruction of Egypt's economy and society, through IMF, World Bank, EU, and the United States. They were destroying Egypt's economy in collaboration with its governments: That's what the Egyptian people revolted against.

And now the new President says in every speech: I know the Egyptian people are not going to forgive me. I'm not going to be here in a few months unless I do something, because the Egyptian people have learned that they don't care who is in power, they will overthrow them if they don't provide jobs, if they don't fix the economy, if they don't provide food.

There's a Vision in Egypt

Now, Egypt is importing 70% of its needs, from food to cars, everything! So the Egyptians are saying, "we are in a terrible situation." *But*, what they now have have a vision of the solution. They have a vision of the future. They are working sometimes on a crisis-management basis, solving problems every week, every month, and then they use a lot of resources to protect the Egyptian pound. The reserves of food, of grain in Egypt is only enough to last to June. After that they are working with Russia, with Belarus, with Ukraine, to get as much grain as possible, because after June there is no bread in Egypt!

But what is new in Egypt? There is a vision. There's a leadership which believes that they can do farm work. They have qualified people. In Egypt, the Egyptian engineers syndicate has 400,000 members! There are 400,000 Egyptian engineers, and they're very well-educated people. But their infrastructure has been destroyed, their currency is under attack. Their vision of what we call "national credit" is not complete, and that's one of the things I tried to intervene on, that Egypt does not need money from Saudi Arabia or the EU or the United States to build the economy, you can do it internally, but you've got to understand the right mechanism. That's how the United States built its economy.

But what is interesting for me, is the future. But, are

Conditions in the Middle East are horrendous. But we are not alone. More than half the world is behind us. There is a new dynamic in the world which China has proven economically, and Russia has proven strategically. Either you join it, or we will all be destroyed.

---

people today working for the future? Or are they crying over spilled milk? And therefore, everybody here,— I mean, we know, and I come from Iraq. I lived through three wars before I left Iraq in 1991, and afterward was the horrendous sanctions in Iraq which destroyed the society. And then there was the invasion of Iraq, and we have had a civil war and religious war, and god knows what.

But, it's not good for my health to think about all the horrible things that have gone on in Iraq. What is good for my health and the health of the Iraqis is if I fight for a world order which can restore Iraq to its greatness. And it's the same thing in Egypt. It's the same thing with Syria, every nation. So the Syrians who are here in Europe, they should fight with *our* ideas to get these ideas on the table everywhere.

We are not alone. We have more than half of the world population and governments behind us. That's what is new in this situation. The Chinese have proven it economically. The Russians have proven it strategically and in military terms. So we have to invest all our energy, all our capabilities to bring into people's minds, whether it's citizens, relatives, people in government, everywhere, that there's an idea, there's a solution, there's a new dynamic in the world. You either join it, or we will all be destroyed.

So, that's my answer.

Celani: There is a microphone here. If you have a question keep it short; if you have a statement, keep it shorter. [laughter]

Question: [The questioner spoke in German, with sequential translation] Since 1960, there's talk about a project Transaqua, but nothing has happened since. So what have the five countries in that region, the LCBC [Lake Chad Basin Commission], what have they done in that period to change the situation? I don't want to be too direct, but I would emphasize that it would be urgent to overcome the bureaucratic problems and really start to work directly on that project, to bring it forward. For that project we have to also bring our people together.

There are a lot of engineers, hydrologists, throughout the whole region of the five respective countries who know how to handle the technical issues. Why haven't you approached the organization of these technicians, these engineers, to really work on the details of that project? And why wasn't the government of the Democratic Republic of Congo been approached to present that project, or whether they had some insight into it?

The LCBC should definitely overcome its bureaucratic approach to that. I think they should definitely work on the hard facts how to implement them. And they also have to internally bring the money together, as Hussein Askary was mentioning with the Suez Canal project as the Egyptian government did it. They should just get their act together to put it nicely.

Celani: Thank you. Does somebody want to answer?

Motion on Lake Chad

Mohammed Bila: Thank you very much. I didn't get your name, maybe later. The biggest problem we're having, is how to run the LCBC. Since the LCBC was created in 1964, most of our projects ... were rejected, due to several reasons, environmental causes, and other reasons.... The idea was to get the financial partners to support the idea. But nobody was willing to.

In 1994, the LCBC initiated a project, mainly financed by the United Nations Environmental Program, that they order a master plan for the Lake Chad Basin. And among these master plans, one of the projects is the feasibility study for water transport. Where would the financing come from? We got financing from the different countries. That idea was rejected, for the same reason that you have environmental impacts, it might be too costly, it's not realistic. But the member-states went ahead to raise the money. They raised $5 million, and then, instead of using the money for the Transaqua study, it was decided that there should be a smaller one.... That study was done between 2008-2011. After a technical feasibility was done, we realized that if we implement that project, we are only getting about half a meter in the southern region of Lake Chad, and probably 1 meter in the northern area of Lake Chad.

So, this is insufficient to raise the Lake Chad level to its normal state. So, these are the problems. And I think what I got from this seminar is that we have to stop looking at it as a project to save the Lake Chad: We should look at it as a project for developing the Central Africa sub-region. [hearty applause] This is a region where you cannot move from the capital, Kinshasa, to another part of the country unless you use a flight, and they have very, very old airplanes in that region. This is a region where there is no infrastructure, no roads, nor electricity, despite having a vast quantity of water. But the biggest part of the country doesn't have electricity. The biggest part of the D.R.C. is cut off. In the Central African Republic it is the same issue: you only have electricity in Bangui, the capital, probably five hours in a day.

So, we have to refocus the project. It is *not* about saving Lake Chad. It is about cooperating, it's about African integration and development of Africa: This is one lesson I'm learning from this.

And the next problem that you raise, what is the role of the D.R.C. government? We had to get the support of Kabila, to give his "no objection" for the study to be done, the initial study. So that means we have to increase our diplomatic approach. I think now we have a better need for union, to have the African Union. So we have to find a way to let the African Union take this as an infrastructure project for Africa. Thus we would be able to get full support from the government of D.R.C.

And most importantly, they shouldn't be listening to those who are emphasizing the impact of the project. We should be listening collectively, we want to raise the standard of living of our people. We want to stop the conflicts, we want to stop the poverty. So this will be the main or key points. How do we finance it? Do we have to put money up from Ethiopia, and also from Egypt? If we really want to do it, we can raise part of the financing internally, and I think this should be a solution.

It's not the way to go forward, but now we have a force, the Lake Chad Basin projects are being a force to do something ... Are our donor partners willing to support us, is what we shall wait and see. [applause]

Peace and Development

Celani: I want to ask something to our friend Ulf Sandmark, but allow me a short introduction. I spoke to Mr. Bila yesterday, and he told me something that shocked me. Because he lives in Germany and in Chad; but he's a Nigerian, so his family and friends are in Nigeria. So he used to travel from Germany and to Nigeria on a distance which here in Europe, I would make in seven hours; it's like going from Wiesbaden to Milan. And he would take a little bit longer, one day, or 12 hours, or whatever; until terrorists came, until Boko Haram came. And that Boko Haram came meant that this road which is the main connection between Chad and Nigeria was totally interrupted, because Boko Haram would come and would kill everybody whom they would meet on this road. This means civilians, this means military, but also commercial traffic.

So there was a total paralysis of commercial exchanges between Chad and Nigeria, with a very strong impact—I mean, not talking about the people who get slaughtered, right? Innocent people—but a total breakdown of food supplies from Chad to Nigeria. And here in Europe we didn't hear anything about this, right? Nobody talks about it, until the situation got reversed.

The situation got reversed when the Lake Chad countries came together and built a multinational force: This is an all-African army. The bulk of this is Nigerian forces, and the commanding general is Nigerian. And for me it's interesting how they succeeded in forming such a multinational force, which is not easy. You have to pull six countries' together and it was not difficult. Until somebody came out and, this is the story the executive secretary told us the other day, and somebody came out within them, and said "But we have already an international body of cooperation among those countries. So let's use this body to be the coordination of a multinational force." And this worked!

So now the multinational force has a political coordination body, which is also the political secretary of the Lake Chad Basin Commission. So the two things, the strategic peace achieving policy and the economic development body come together. And now the situation's been totally reversed because this army is effective! This army is destroying Boko Haram. Boko Haram has lost the capability to fight on the ground in a battle. They have two main terrorist centers, one which has been isolated, and now they want to isolate the second one which is around Lake Chad. This is not the story, I won't go into details, but what this showed to me is that, if you have a common interest for development, then peace is easier!

Why is China in Africa?

Celani: I have a question now for the General Consul of Ethiopia, because you might have noticed a general line of the European media and general media on China, and China's activity in Africa. So this general line says, "China is in Africa to rape raw materials, land, etc." Now, I would like you tell us what is your experience, is this true or not, at least in your case?

And the second question: You mentioned the fact that the economic relationships between Germany and Ethiopia could improve a lot, and I would like you then to tell us a little bit more, what could or should Germany do? what are the steps. what are the concrete policies, that you would like to have from Germany, or with Germany?

Consul General Mehreteab Mulugeta Haile: Thank you. Well, when it comes to the Chinese activity in Africa, and China's activity particularly in Ethiopia, just to answer in brief your question from the experience of Ethiopia, I can say that the Chinese are not in Ethiopia for raw materials, because we don't have any raw materials. We don't have oil, we don't have other natural resources which the Chinese have been accused of looking for and coming for these raw materials in Ethiopia.

The Chinese are there as development partners in Ethiopia. They are collaborating with our government, by financing different development projects. As I said earlier, they are in Ethiopia helping to develop roads, they are constructing different road projects, they are engaging in the construction of highway projects, they are engaged in the development of our telecommunication mobile internet, they are financing different industrial zones.

So, in Ethiopia, the Chinese are helping the government to come out of poverty. The government has a plan for bringing Ethiopia out of poverty, and the Chinese are there as a partner of development. So I can say that the Chinese have no need to get raw materials, but they are there in financing different development projects.

When it comes to Germany, as I said in my presentation, Ethiopia and Germany established diplomatic relations in 1905. And over the last 111 years, there has been a good relationship between Germany and Ethiopia. The German government, through GTZ [German Technical Cooperation Agency] has been helping in different development activities being carried out in especially in the education sector by building different technical and vocational institutions, by bringing students to Germany and giving training. There are a lot of Ethiopians who have been trained in Germany.

But, when it comes to the current development scenario in Ethiopia, where we are encouraging the private business, where we are encouraging investment, where we are encouraging trade, we are not seeing that much activity by the German private sector. The Germans are not coming to Ethiopia with investment. The Germans are not trading in Ethiopia, with Ethiopia as we would like to see. Of course, the Germans buy our coffee; almost 30% of Ethiopian export coffee comes to Germany, but there are a lot of products which can go to Germany, in addition to coffee.

So, when I say we need a lot of cooperation, what I mean is that the German government should encourage the German private sector to come to Ethiopia and Africa to invest, rather than sit and wait for others' initiatives. We found out that most German companies are really conservative when it comes to Africa. They prefer to invest in Eastern Europe, Southeast Asia, and South Asia.

But as they said, the Twenty-first Century is the century for Africa: Africa is developing and there are a lot of opportunities in development and trade. That's what I mean, that in addition to the development assistance it is providing, the German government should encourage the private sector to come into Africa as investors and trade partners. Thank you. [applause]

Celani: Yes, we have someone from the audience.
Question: Hello… We have heard a lot today about concepts and good approaches and doing something in Africa, having the Silk Road plan, all of which is good. On the other side, we have heard about the crisis which is coming close now. My question is, what is the timing? Where do we stand in these various approaches and how much time do we have? I mean, things can happen, also here in Frankfurt any day, as we have seen in Brussels yesterday.

The Urgency of This Mission

Zepp-LaRouche: I think it's very good that you put the focus back on the urgency, because that is what it is. If it were only about the New Silk Road conception, the World Land-Bridge becoming a reality, we could be very optimistic, because that's on the table More and more countries are joining, it's a very attractive model. It brings favors as the General Consul from Ethiopia just was—I think it was very valuable that you said that, because a country that has no raw materials, no oil, nobody can accuse China of being out for [its own interest.

So if it were only about the Silk Road, I think it's a winning development and it would be perfect. The only problem is that the trans-Atlantic financial system is so bankrupt. You see, in 2008 Lehman Brothers happened. We had the potential meltdown of the system and there was after Lehman and AIG, there were a couple of weeks where everybody was completely panicked and thought "this is it." Even Sarkozy was talking about the "need to have a New Bretton Wood system," but that only lasted a few days and weeks, and by the time you had the first G20 summit in Washington on Nov. 15, 2008, they all had basically agreed, "no, no, fundamental reform, we will go for bail-out," and you had all these packages, bail-out packages, the Federal Reserve spent altogether spent, I think at the high point about $30 billion to bail out the banks. They put through Dodd-Frank to prevent Glass-Steagall, they had the Vickers Commission, they had all kinds of proposals about how to maintain the high speculation system by throwing confetti into the eyes of the people so they wouldn't see it.

This then was followed by the bail-in policy. You remember the Cyprus crisis about three years ago, where they just expropriated the accounts of the people who had savings accounts or bonds in the banks, and that led to about 60% expropriation of people in Cyprus. And now, we are in a situation where the too-big-to-fail banks are about between 40% and 80% larger than in 2008; the outstanding derivatives debt is $2 quadrillion; and at the recent Davos Economic Forum, the former chief economist of the Bank for International Settlements, William White, said that the situation of the debt is such that it's not payable, and that therefore, there are only two choices: One is an uncontrolled collapse, which leads to chaos, or an orderly reorganization, and he used the fact that in all great religions in the last 5,000 years, you had something called the "Jubilee," in other words, when the system becomes too indebted, you just write the debt off and you start anew. So that's one way of doing it.

You also could have a London debt conference like in 1953 concerning Germany, or even better, you have

to go back to exactly what Franklin D. Roosevelt did with the Glass-Steagall banking separation law in 1933.

Now, in the United States you obviously have a crisis. You have something which I don't even want to find a right name for it, it's called "Trump." This is a monstrosity, who says the most unbelievable things,

---

Now the too-big-to-fail banks are 40 to 80 percent larger than in 2008. The debt is not payable. There are two choices: An uncontrolled, chaotic collapse, or an orderly reorganization.

---

and I think some newspaper just recognized his vocabulary is that of a second-grade pupil, his style is that of a mixture between Dracula and Mussolini, and a drug addict, a mafioso,— I don't know, but it's an unbelievable perspective.

But however, it's not a crash that could only happen in the next year: It's going to happen now. As a matter of fact, the urgency of the matter is that we're sitting on such a volcano that the financial system could evaporate as we speak here. When Draghi was announcing a zero interest rate, negative interest rates for banks which park money in the ECB, this is the end of the rope! Because the Bank of Japan, the ECB, the Bank of Norway, all went to zero interest rate, and that was intended to get the economy going somehow to further investment, and the opposite happened. What you have right now, is that the key currencies are in a competitive devaluation spiral, without effect. You know, this is a classical breakdown crisis.

And then at the same press conference, Draghi was asked by a journalist, what about "helicopter money"? Now, helicopter money was introduced as an idea by the former head of the Federal Reserve Ben Bernanke, who said famously, some 10, 15 years ago, he said, before we allow the complete meltdown of the financial system, we will put helicopters over the cities and just throw as much money out as is required. So when Draghi was asked, "what about helicopter money?" He said, "this is a very interesting concept and we are discussing it." And then, last Saturday, there must have been some background discussion, I only saw an interview by the head of the Bundesbank Jens Weidmann, who said that "helicopter money is a terrible idea, it completely goes beyond the mandate of the central banks, because it's a gigantic redistribution, from poor to rich, and that must be decided by the governments and the parliaments.

We are in such a dramatic situation, that I can only repeat, we have to shake up people in Europe right now. Because you know, the only way that this thing could be solved is very easy. Now, you saw the cartoon with Mrs. Merkel making the little steps, where the next little step brings her over the cliff. The only way how this thing could be saved, easily, is if we create some pressure in the population, where Merkel will be finished if she continues with her Turkey policy, because this will backfire, it will not function. Just imagine: I was in New Delhi at this Raisina Dialogue conference, and one of the panels was "On the Failure of the EU Concerning the Refugee Policy." And the whole world is asking, where are the moral values of the EU if they are treating refugees like that? There was a complete common understanding that the EU is completely bankrupt.

Easy to Solve

Now, if this woman wants to solve the situation, it would be very easy. If I were in the Chancellor's Office, I would make a TV address and I would say, "I just talked to Putin, Xi Jinping, Modi, Rouhani, el-Sisi, and we decided that we will develop Southwest Asia with a Silk Road Marshall Plan." All the neighbors get together, we all have a security interest that terrorism must stop, and therefore, we have a plan that we not only reconstruct Syria and Iraq, but we will, together,— because infrastructure is not something you can just develop, a bridge in Syria, and road in Iraq. You have to have a complete, overall plan, like we do for Europe all the time.

And if you look at our World Land-Bridge report, we had proposed a development plan in 2012 for South Europe, because it was clear the Troika policy would not work, and we took one concept which was from the Transport Minister, the "*Verkehrswegeplan,*" that is, a "general design for transportation infrastructure" of the European Transport Ministers from a conference they had in Crete in 1994, where they developed the idea, or decided to have 10 development corridors for the Balkans, for Southern Italy, for Spain. And this is ready, it could be started tomorrow. But because the Troika believes in saving the banks and not going into infrastructure, this has never been carried out, even if a lot of

feasibility studies have been done. For example, for the tunnel under the Strait of Gibraltar, between the government of Spain and the government of Morocco, a state treaty exists to build this tunnel. And a Swiss firm has made a feasibility study that it would work perfectly. It's an engineering project that could happen tomorrow. So a lot of aspects are ready in the drawers, and could start tomorrow!

But what we need is to have a general discussion in European media, in European blogs. People who have organizations, such as being members of the Rotary Club or members of the Chamber of Commerce, or they're members of other associations, and you have to fight to get this perspective known! Austria is much further ahead of Germany because they now have a whole bunch of articles in the official newspapers of the foreign trade associations, saying it would be to the benefit of Austria to work with the Silk Road. China is building a railroad from Vienna to Budapest, and this is in the interest of Austria that this be extended to the Balkans. And we need to mobilize! This is not a moment where we can be complacent, because we are sitting on a complete powder keg.

The solution would be very easy: We need Glass-Steagall, we need to end the casino economy, and then we need to have a credit system, join the organizations like AIIB, the New Development Bank, or go back to the Kreditanstalt für Wiederaufbau which did finance the Marshall Plan in Germany after the Second World War. We can finance all of these projects.

The solution is very, very simple; what is lacking is the mobilization of the population to put fire behind the behinds of such people. I always said, where there is no reason you can appeal to, there is still the policy of the burning shirt. When people feel that their shirt is burning, they get up and they start moving. And in that sense, as tragic as the situation is with the refugee crisis, I still believe that it is the game-changer, because it gives us the opportunity to tell people, "Look, we have neglected Africa for 50 years." We condoned the IMF conditionalities which lowered the living standard of an entire continent so that it *could not* develop!

This is now haunting us. And in the same way, we condoned lies, which led to wars. In Iraq there was no weapons of mass destruction. It was lies concerning Qaddafi, it was lies concerning Assad. You heard several people speaking about that. Assad had a good, functioning country: it was a secular country, religions worked together peacefully. In the case of Libya, you don't have to be a friend of Qaddafi, but Qaddafi was investing in infrastructure, not only in Libya but in other African countries!

So we have to start to dismantle these lies and we have to put the alternative on the table. And I can only say, the fact now that we have this report in English, in Chinese, in Arabic, and we will soon be producing it in Russian. It's being translated into Korean; we are negotiating with people in Japan to publish it. And I think we need to publish it in Germany! [applause]

I mean, this is a blueprint for the reconstruction of the world economy, and we should get papers to write reviews about it, to just talk about it, so that it exists as an alternative. And then have a lobby or a mass movement—I don't care what you call it—but the solution is there, it's just not known well enough. [applause]

Celani: Well, everybody's happy, I believe? Mr. Stalleicher?

Joseph Stalleicher: I just have a question for the Italians. Since you had the Renaissance, you had Brunelleschi. What do you think about this? You are the country in Europe that had this experience of getting out of the Dark Age. So, I think the kernel of this conference is that we have to have this optimistic vision. So I just want to ask you as an Italian what you think about this?

Marcello Vicchi: My impression is that we must be optimists. Because being pessimistic is too easy. [laughter] Especially today. But in the last period that we were [working at] Bonifica, always, I repeated to my collaborators, "We are paid to be optimists, and not to be pessimists. We are *paid* for this!" at that time. Now...? [applause]

HELGA ZEPP-LAROUCHE'S CLOSING STATEMENT

Europe Must Regain Classical Culture

I would just like to say one final thing: What people don't know is that in China, Confucianism is very much alive. China is doing the things it does because the present Chinese leadership is not so much communist, but much more Confucianist, and they're putting a lot of emphasis on education, on the development of the minds of the young people, on excellence in creativity, on moving forward.

We have lost that spirit in Europe. We are not thinking about Classical culture. The only reason why people are afraid of foreigners is because we have lost our culture!

You know the famous discussion about *Leitkultur* is a joke because we have no more consciousness—I mean, we are one of the richest cultures of all the countries of the world, the German Classical period. But is it the live culture in our population? It's not!

We have always said that one can only solve this problem by combining economic development with a cultural Renaissance. This is why we're putting a lot of emphasis on Verdi tuning, we want to go back to the Verdi tuning and bel canto singing; we emphasise Furtwängler; we emphasise the great German *Lied*, be-

cause we have to have this combination, we have to find a way to get back to the humanistic ideas of Schiller. I'm the president of the Schiller Institute because I believe that we need the image of man of Friedrich Schiller.

It's therefore not just a question of economics, it's not just a question of infrastructure, but it's a question of building a Renaissance. And I think if we do our job right, we can revive the German Classical tradition, the Italian Classical tradition, we can relate to Confucianism in China, we can go to all the high points of all the cultures and have a dialogue among the Gupta period, the Vedic writings in India, the best traditions of Persia, of Africa. There were periods during which Ethiopia was one of the greatest cultures of mankind! Many schools of thought say that the entirety of human development comes from Ethiopia.

So we have to understand that we either go under as a barbaric culture, which we are on the verge of doing, or we revive the best traditions of all civilizations and have a dialogue among them, and make a new Renaissance out of that. And that is a joyful perspective, and I want to advise and invite all of you to join it.

LINK WEST CHINA TO SOUTH ASIA AND THE ARABIAN SEA

China's Grand Plan Is On the Move
PART I

by Ramtanu Maitra

March 26—In July 2013, China and Pakistan signed a landmark agreement which would enable China to construct an economic corridor linking the Chinese city of Kashgar in Western China's Xinjiang province to Pakistan's southwestern coastal port, Gwadar. The economic corridor, named the China-Pakistan Economic Corridor (CPEC), will run through Gilgit-Baltistan in the north, a part of the disputed Jammu and Kashmir, and through all four Pakistani provinces to the Arabian Sea in the south. The entire project is expected to take 15 years to complete, but when completed, it could open up enormous economic prospects by interlinking China with South Asia, Central Asia, and Iran.

It will also enable China to bring in oil and gas from the Persian Gulf to develop its western region and avoid further crowding of the already overcrowded Malacca Strait that connects the Indian Ocean to the South China Sea to the east. Gwadar is just 400 km from the Strait of Hormuz, a major world oil supply line, and 1,500 km from Kashgar, China.

As a result, when the CPEC route becomes operational, a significant part of China's oil imports

from the Persian Gulf, which amount to about 60% of China's overall oil import, only needs to travel a total distance of 2,000 km from the Strait of Hormuz to enter West China, as opposed to 12,000 km of maritime distance from the Strait of Hormuz to the

eastern Chinese port of Shanghai via the Strait of Malacca.

It is reasonable that a project which would require a vast amount of capital and a huge manpower investment, will be done in phases. Media reports indicate the first phase of the economic corridor will focus on developing energy and infrastructure projects. The estimated cost would be close to $46 billion, although cost overruns are generally expected. China's state-owned banks will finance Chinese companies to fund, build, and operate these energy and infrastructure projects in Pakistan over the next six years, according to a Reuters report, Nov. 21, 2014.

Of that amount, $33.8 billion will be invested in various energy projects and $11.8 billion in infrastructure projects, such as upgrading railroads, building motorways, and even setting up a desalination plant. According to Reuters, under the CPEC agreement, $15.5 billion worth of coal, wind, solar, and hydro energy projects will add 10,400 megawatts of energy to the national grid of power-starved Pakistan. An additional 6,120 megawatts will be added to the national grid at a cost of $18.2 billion by 2021.

The agreement also includes major upgrades to Pakistan's transport infrastructure, such as:

• Extension of the Karakorum Highway from Havelian in the Abbottabad District in Pakistan's western province of Khyber-Pakhtoonkhwa to Thakot, a small town in Khyber-Pakhtoonkhwa, a distance of about 133 km

• Construction of a 387 km six-lane highway from Sukkur (in the province of Sindh) to Multan (in the province of Punjab), a section of the 1,148 km Karachi-Lahore Motorway

• The Gwadar Port East Bay Expressway Project to connect the port with Pakistan's M-8 motorway and N-85 highway, linking Gwadar directly to Ratodero/Sukkur in the province of Sindh, and Quetta, the capital of Balochistan province, through Turbat, Panjgur, and Sohrab

• Building an international airport at Gwadar.

Arguably the most important element for China in financing this vast CPEC project is the development of Gwadar Port, the southern pivot of CPEC. Gwadar is an all-weather, deep-sea port situated on the Makran coast of Pakistan's Balochistan province at the junction of the Arabian Sea and the Gulf of Oman, the western extension of the Arabian Sea that leads to the Persian Gulf. It is located 460 km west of Karachi, Pakistan's largest city, main port, and commercial hub, and is situated approximately 75 km east of Pakistan's border with Iran.

From China's viewpoint, development of Gwadar and the economic corridor through Pakistan would not only enable it to develop a direct transportation artery to West China, but it would cut down oil importation costs significantly.

The development of Gwadar Port has been in the offing for years, but its development was of secondary import to cash-starved Pakistan. Since the economic rise of China, and its keenness to develop western China, the building up of Gwadar Port received an impetus.

The development of the port is being done in two phases. With the help of the Chinese, the first phase began in 2002. The most important elements of the first phase of development include:

• The building of three multipurpose berths, each 602 meters long

• Developing a 4.5 km approach channel, of 11.5 to 12.5 meters depth

• Building port infrastructure and port handling equipment.

The first phase was completed and inaugurated in 2008.

Following the completion of the first phase of the project, the Port of Singapore Authority (PSA) was hired for the management of the Port. In May 2013, Gwadar Port Authority handed over the management to China Overseas Port Holding Company (COPHC) for a lease of 40 years.

The $840 million second phase of the port development has begun and is undertaken with $500 million financing by China, and is now in progress. The key elements of the second phase of development consist of constructing:

• Four container berths

• One bulk cargo terminal

• One grain terminal

• One roll off-roll on (Ro-Ro) terminal

• Two oil terminals to accommodate 20,000 DWT ships each.

The approach channel will be dredged to 14.5 meters depth.

To follow: Part II. CPEC: A Cornucopia for Pakistan in the Making.

www.ingramcontent.com/pod-product-compliance
Lightning Source LLC
Chambersburg PA
CBHW081604280526
45788CB00011B/3551